海外藏中国艺术品
OVERSEAS CHINESE ART SELECTION

绘画卷·明(三)

PAINTINGS·MING (3)

本书编写组 编著
Compiled by Editorial Team

郭怀宇 本卷主编
Edited by Guo Huaiyu

NEWSTAR PRESS
新星出版社

图书在版编目（CIP）数据

海外藏中国艺术品．绘画卷．明．三：汉英对照 / 郭怀宇主编；本书编写组编著．-- 北京：新星出版社，2024.12

ISBN 978-7-5133-5444-8

Ⅰ．①海… Ⅱ．①郭… ②本… Ⅲ．①中国画－中国－明代－图录 Ⅳ．① K870.2

中国国家版本馆 CIP 数据核字（2024）第 056604 号

海外藏中国艺术品 绘画卷·明（三）

本书编写组 编 著
郭 怀 宇 本卷主编

责任编辑 李文彧　**特约编辑** 丁文文
英文审校 韩 华　**责任校对** 刘 义
装帧设计 冷暖儿　**责任印制** 李珊珊

出 版 人 马汝军
出版发行 新星出版社
（北京市西城区车公庄大街丙 3 号楼 8001　100044）
网　　址 www.newstarpress.com
法律顾问 北京市岳成律师事务所
印　　刷 河北尚唐印刷包装有限公司
开　　本 889mm×1194mm　1/16
印　　张 13.5
字　　数 338 千字
版　　次 2024 年 12 月第 1 版　2024 年 12 月第 1 次印刷
书　　号 ISBN 978-7-5133-5444-8
定　　价 298.00 元

总机：010-88310888　传真：010-65270449　销售中心：010-88310811

出版说明

按中国文物学会统计，鸦片战争以来流失海外的中国文物超过一千万件。这些文物是中国文物重要而特殊的组成部分，除其历史、文化、艺术等方面价值，更因其所凝结的民族情感而备受各界关注。

近年来，中国政府积极推动文物追索，国内外学界也涌现出一批新的研究成果，文物流失研究方兴未艾。但受诸多因素限制，海外文物归国面临着许多实际困难，能追回的仍只是很少一部分。在此情况下，加强中外合作、开展联合研究，通过出版、数字化等方式让更多人有机会了解相关资料和研究成果，成了推动流失文物"活起来"、促进中华文化海外传播的一条可行路径。在国内外专家学者、文博机构等的支持下，新星出版社推出这套《海外藏中国艺术品》，希望能为广大读者及学者提供一套可资观赏、查阅和研究的参考读物。

《海外藏中国艺术品》出版之际，我们尤其希望通过这套书向林树中先生致敬。林树中先生自20世纪80年代起，花费近20年时间，自费走遍40多个国家和地区的200多所博物馆，呕心沥血、锲而不舍，记录了大量海外藏中国文物资料，编纂出版了《海外藏中国历代名画》，成为这一领域具有重大影响力的开创性成果。2013年，新星出版社联手林树中教授共同策划了《海外藏中国艺术品》项目，旨在全面整理他对流失海外的绘画、雕塑、书法、工艺品的丰富记录和研究成果。不幸的是，筹备工作开始不久，林树中教授因病辞世，这给整理与编纂工作带来巨大挑战，出版计划也因此被迫中断。

《海外藏中国艺术品》编纂出版的两大关键因素是专家学者的专业把关和海外藏品的图片授权。在重启并继续推动项目的过程中，我们重新组建了国内外专家组成的编纂团队，英国独角兽公司则协调许多知名博物馆向我们开放图片授权。合法取得文物图片使用授权后，编纂团队对入选文物加以鉴别与甄选，按时代顺序进行分卷、编排，并对文物中英文定名、创作时代、创作者、材质、规格等馆藏信息进行逐一确认。

《海外藏中国艺术品》共计20卷，收录文物2279件，来自海外33家知名博物馆，涵盖了铜器（2册）、陶瓷（3册）、书法（3册）、绘画（11册）和造像（1册）五大门类。

此次出版的《海外藏中国艺术品》因故未能收录金银器、玉器、服饰等艺术门类。我们愿以《海外藏中国艺术品》的出版为契机，努力搭建研究交流和成果出版发布平台，期待与国内外有关各方携手，共同推进流失文物领域相关工作，为中华优秀传统文化传承发展和中华文化国际传播作出新贡献。

囿于出版者水平，书中难免缺漏错讹之处，敬请专家、读者指正。

Preface

According to statistics from the Chinese Society of Cultural Relics, over ten million Chinese cultural relics have been dispersed overseas since the Opium War in the mid-19th century. They represent an important and unique part of China's cultural heritage. Beyond their historical, cultural, and artistic value, they are also of great interest to all sectors of society due to the national sentiments they embody.

In recent years, the Chinese government has been actively engaging in the recovery of Chinese cultural relics, and domestic and international academia has seen a surge in new research, making the study of the loss of Chinese cultural relics a burgeoning field. However, practical challenges have constrained the repatriation efforts, resulting in the recovery of only a small fraction of these relics. In light of this, it has become a feasible approach to enhance visibility and awareness of these artifacts through strengthened international cooperation, joint research, and the dissemination of materials and findings via publications and digitalization. With the support of domestic and international experts, scholars, cultural institutions, and museums, New Star Press has published the *Overseas Chinese Art Selection* series. This series aims to provide reference materials for readers and scholars to appreciate, consult, and study.

Upon the publication of this series, we would like to take this opportunity to pay tribute to Mr. Lin Shuzhong. Beginning in the 1980s, Lin devoted nearly two decades visiting over 200 museums in more than 40 countries and regions at his own expense. With remarkable dedication and perseverance, he documented a vast amount of information about Chinese cultural relics overseas and compiled and published *Famous Chinese Paintings Abroad*, which has become a groundbreaking work with significant influence in this field. In 2013, New Star Press collaborated with Professor Lin on *Overseas Chinese Art Selection*, aiming to comprehensively organize his extensive records and research on paintings, sculptures, calligraphy, and crafts lost overseas. Tragically, shortly after the preparatory work began, he passed away due to illness, presenting significant challenges to the project's continuation. As a result, the publication plan had to be suspended.

The successful compilation and publication of *Overseas Chinese Art Selection* depended on two critical factors: the professional scrutiny of experts and scholars and the license to use images granted by overseas museums. In the process of restarting the project, we set up a new compilation team composed of local and international experts. UK-based Unicorn Publishing Group LLP coordinated with many renowned overseas museums to secure permissions for image use. After legally obtaining their permissions, the compilation team appraised and selected artifacts, organized them into different categories and in chronological order, and confirmed collection information for each piece, including Chinese and English names, the time of creation, the artist's name, material, specifications, and other relevant information.

Overseas Chinese Art Selection consists of 20 volumes, with 2,279 cultural relics from 33 renowned museums overseas, covering five major categories: bronzes (two volumes), ceramics (three volumes), calligraphy (three volumes), paintings (11 volumes), and sculptures (one volume).

Categories such as gold and silver wares, jade wares, and costumes are not included. We hope this publication will help build a platform for research exchanges and publication of research findings. We are looking forward to working together with partners at home and abroad to jointly pursue initiatives related to lost Chinese cultural treasures, and contribute to the inheritance and development of China's excellent traditional culture and a wider knowledge of Chinese culture globally.

Despite our best efforts, errors and inaccuracies may be present due to the limitations of the publisher's expertise. We kindly invite experts and readers to point them out for further improvement.

凡例

一、《海外藏中国艺术品》绘画卷收录了宋、元、明、清代共 1178 件画作，每件画作由图片和中英文基本信息两部分组成。

二、本卷中画作依照时代分册：宋代 2 册，元代 1 册，明、清代各 4 册，共计 11 册。

三、本卷中具体画作顺序基本依照画家生卒年先后编排，同时兼顾风格、流派等相关因素。同一画家的画作如有准确年款，则依年款先后编排，无准确年款的画作基本按立轴、手卷、册页、扇面形制依序编排；传为某画家的画作，均编排在该画家画作最后。佚名画作均编排于各时代最后，并依人物、山水、花鸟等门类略作分类。

四、本卷中已有中文定名的画作名称，与官网名称不一致的，均依已有中文定名。

五、本卷中以朝代标明画作的时代信息，其相应的英文表述，统一注明朝代和具体起止时间，如“Ming dynasty (1368—1644)”。部分画作有准确年款，均注明。

六、本卷中画作的材质基本统一为纸本水墨、纸本设色、绢本水墨、绢本设色、绫本水墨、绫本设色六种，对应英文为 ink on paper，ink and color on paper，ink on silk，ink and color on silk，ink on satin，ink and color on satin。将 ink and touches of color on silk；ink，color，gold and silver on silk；ink and color on gold-flecked paper；ink and pale color on paper 等统一为以上相应材质。

七、本卷中画作的尺寸基本为画面尺寸，并注明了画面纵、横尺寸，对应英文为 H、W。

八、本卷充分尊重各海外博物馆的要求，将每幅画作的出处和图片版权信息均详细列出。但因该信息并非对画作本身的描述，故未翻译成中文。其中个别博物馆或美术馆，如大阪市立美术馆，未提供该信息，因此未收录。

Guide to the Reader

i. The paintings volume of *Overseas Chinese Art Selection* contains 1178 pieces of paintings from the Song (960-1279), Yuan (1271-1368), Ming (1368-1644) and Qing (1644-1911) dynasties. Each piece is accompanied by basic information in Chinese and English.

ii. The paintings are presented chronologically in eleven volumes, of which two volumes are for paintings from Song Dynasty, one volume including those of Yuan Dynasty, four volumes for those of Ming Dynasty and another four for paintings from Qing Dynasty.

iii. The order of the paintings within each dynasty generally follows the period of time when the artists lived, taking the artistic styles, genres, etc. into consideration. Paintings by the same artist are primarily sorted in accordance with the exact chronology information when known; otherwise, they are arranged in accordance with the form of the paintings, namely in the order of handing scroll, handscroll, album leaf, fan paintings. Paintings attributed to an uncertain artist, are placed at the very end of the composer's paintings. Anonymous paintings are sorted at the end of paintings of each dynasty in this volume in accordance with the category of figure, scenery, birds and flowers, etc.

iv. The established Chinese names of those paintings which may be given different names by the official website will be retained in this volume.

v. The era of the paintings is marked by the dynasty in the volume. Both the dynasty and specific starting and ending years of the dynasties are indicated in the English description, such as "Ming Dynasty (1368-1644)". The specific creating time of some paintings is already known, which has been presented clearly.

vi. The materials used in the paintings in this volume are primarily summarized into six types: namely ink on paper, ink and color on paper, ink on silk, ink and color on silk, ink on stain, ink and color on stain. While there are numerous varitions, such as ink and touches of color on silk; ink, color, gold and silver on silk; ink and color on gold-flecked paper; ink and pale color on paper; etc. These have been standardized to the above categories for consistency.

vii. Dimensions in the basic information of this volume primarily represent the size of the painting's image, with vertical measurements denoted by 'H' and horizontal measurements by 'W'.

viii. This volume fully respects the requirements of overseas museums, the credit line and image copyright of paintings provided by the museums have been listed in details. However, since such information is not a description of the paintings themselves, it is presented only in English. Some museums or galleries, such as The Osaka City Museum of Fine Arts, do not provide those information of the paintings when displaying them, therefore such information of some paintings is omitted here.

目　录

CONTENTS

明（三）

The Ming Dynasty（3）

199. 石泉图..003
Waterfall

200. 仿文徵明山水图..............................004
Landscape After Wen Zhengming

201. 初夏山斋图....................................005
Mountain Studio in Early Summer

202. 潇湘八景图....................................007
Eight Views of Xiao and Xiang

203. 寒山访友图....................................010
Returning with Crane on Snowy River

204. 高山图..011
High Mountains

205. 寒林钟馗图....................................012
Zhong Kui, Demon Queller

206. 为文徵明作山水图...........................014
Suzhou Temple Garden

207. 抑斋曾叔祖八十五龄寿像..................015
Portrait of Artist's Great-granduncle Yizhai at Age of Eighty-five

208. 老妇像..016
Portrait of Old Lady

209. 萧翼赚兰亭图.................................017
Xiao Yi Obtaining Lanting Preface from Biancai

210. 仿北苑山水图.................................018
Landscape After Dong Yuan

211. 牧牛图..019
Boy on Water Buffalo

212. 田家春斗图....................................021
Farmers Fighting in Springtime

213. 花鸟图..022
Bird on Flowering Branch

214. 杏花双禽图....................................023
Birds, Rocks and Flowering Prunus

215. 秋江图..025
River Landscape

216. 墨兰图..027
Orchids

217. 万古春风图....................................028
Spring Breeze of Myriad Pasts

218. 千山雪霁图....................................029
Thousand Peaks After Snowfall

219. 山水图..030
Landscape

220. 湖州十八景图.................................031
Eighteen Views of Huzhou Yutai Peak

221. 仿黄公望山水图..............................036
Landscape After Huang Gongwang

222. 荷塘花鸟图....................................037
Birds by Lotus Pond

223. 竹石水仙图....................................038
Bamboo, Rock, and Narcissus

224. 菊石图..039
Chrysanthemums and Rock

225. 白描罗汉图....................................041
Baimiao Arhats

226. 浔阳送客图....................................044
Song of Lute

227. 天都晓日图....................................045
Morning Sun over Heavenly Citadel Peak

228. 十六罗汉图....................................047
Sixteen Luohans

229. 翠壁丹枫图....................................051
Green Cliff with Red Maples

230. 五百罗汉图......................................053
Five Hundred Arhats

231. 荆溪招隐图......................................061
Invitation to Reclusion at Jingxi

232. 青弁图..064
Qingbian

233. 仿倪瓒松亭秋色图..............................065
Pavilion Under Pine Trees in Autumn After Ni Zan

234. 山水图..066
Steep Mountains and Silent Waters

235. 仿古山水图......................................067
Landscapes After Old Masters

236. 建溪山水图......................................080
Reminiscence of Jian River

237. 仿董源溪山樾馆图..............................081
Shaded Dwellings Among Streams and Mountains After Dong Yuan

238. 仿巨然山水图..................................083
Landscape After Ju Ran and Calligraphy

239. 盘谷序书画合璧图..............................087
Calligraphy and Painting Based on Han Yu's Preface to Li Yuan Retreats to Pangu

240. 江山秋霁图......................................091
River and Mountains on Clear Autumn Day

241. 仿古山水图......................................093
Landscapes and Poems After Masters

242. 墨梅图..097
Cut Branch of Blossoming Plum

243. 仿古山水图......................................099
Landscapes After Old Masters

244. 云山平远图......................................109
Expansive Views of Clouds and Mountains

245. 仿文徵明山水图................................114
Landscape After Wen Zhengming

246. 濯足图..115
Recluse Washing His Feet in Stream

247. 抚琴图..116
Scholar Playing Qin

248. 乔松磐石图......................................117
Lofty Pines and Great Rock

249. 山水二帧..118
Two Landscapes

250. 竹院逢僧图......................................119
Scholar and Monk in Zhuyuan Buddhist Cloister

251. 溪山无尽图......................................121
Streams and Mountains Without End

252. 墨竹图..124
Bamboo

253. 疏林小景图......................................125
Landscape

254. 溪山村舍图......................................126
Landscape

255. 踈林远山图......................................127
Thin Forest and Distant Mountains

256. 秋窗读易图......................................129
Mountain and Stream in Autumn

257. 仿古山水图......................................132
Landscapes After Old Masters

258. 墨竹图..133
Bamboo

259. 秋林远岫图......................................134
Distant Peaks beyond Autumn Grove

260. 山水图..137
Landscape

261. 山水花鸟图......................................139
Landscapes, Flowers and Birds

262. 岩栖思访图......................................147
Meditative Visit to Mountain Retreat: In Picture and in Words

263. 秋景图..148
Autumn Landscape

264. 竹石梧桐图......................................149
Wutong Tree, Bamboo and Rock

265. 山水图..150
River and Mountain Landscape

266. 梅花图..151
Branch of Blossoming Plum

267. 江山卧游图......................................153
Dream Journey Among Rivers and Mountains

268. 江山梦游图......................................157
Dream Journey Among Rivers and Mountains

269. 青谿卧游图......161
Dream Landscape

270. 清溪入画图......162
Reflections in Clear Stream

271. 临王蒙溪桥玩月图......163
Enjoying Moon: Landscape After Wang Meng

272. 延陵琴瀑图......165
Portrait of Wu Yihan

273. 仿关仝山溪待渡图......166
Waiting for Ferry After Guan Tong

274. 嵩山高图......167
Lofty Mount Song

275. 春江渔隐图......168
Hermit-fisherman on Spring River

276. 仿宋元山水图......169
Landscapes After Song and Yuan Masters

277. 仿高克恭云林秋霁图......181
Landscape After Gao Kegong

278. 仿王蒙山水图......182
Landscape After Wang Meng

279. 仿赵孟頫山水图......183
Landscape After Zhao Mengfu

280. 冬日山居图......184
Thatched Huts Among Ridges in Winter

281. 秋山图......185
Autumn Landscape

282. 仿李唐山水图......186
Landscape After Li Tang

283. 楚山秋霁图......187
Clearing Autumn Mists in Chu Mountains

284. 论道图......188
Conversation

285. 红友图......189
Red Friend

286. 仿李成山水图......190
Autumn colors at Mountain Villa After Li Cheng

287. 仿王维山水图......191
Landscape After Wang Wei

288. 桃园春色图......192
Peach Blossom Spring

289. 仿巨然山水图......193
Landscape After Ju Ran

290. 仿古山水图......195
Landscape After Old Masters

291. 秋江落照图......200
Setting Sun on Autumn River

292. 许旌阳移居图......201
Xu Jingyang Moving His Family

293. 洗象图......202
Grooming Elephant

版权支持......203
Image Contributors

编辑、出版人员......205
Editorial Staff

明（三）

The Ming Dynasty (3)

199. 石泉图

Waterfall

明嘉靖三十八年（公元1559年）
居节
绢本水墨
立轴
纵110.5、横24.8厘米
大都会艺术博物馆

Ming dynasty (1368–1644), dated 1559
Ju Jie
Ink on silk
Hanging scroll
H×W : 110.5×24.8 cm
The Metropolitan Museum of Art
John Stewart Kennedy Fund, 1913

200. 仿文徵明山水图

明隆庆二年（公元1568年）
居节
纸本水墨
立轴
纵88.3、横29.1厘米
耶鲁大学艺术博物馆

Landscape After Wen Zhengming

Ming dynasty (1368–1644), dated 1568
Ju Jie
Ink on paper
Hanging scroll
H×W : 88.3×29.1 cm
The Yale University Art Gallery
Leonard C. Hanna, Jr., Class of 1913, Fund; Mrs. Paul Moore Fund; and Anonymous Oriental Purchase Fund

201. 初夏山斋图

Mountain Studio in Early Summer

明万历六年（公元1578年）
居节
绢本设色
立轴
纵112.1、横31.6厘米
东京国立博物馆

Ming dynasty (1368–1644), dated 1578
Ju Jie
Ink and color on silk
Hanging scroll
H×W : 112.1×31.6 cm
The Tokyo National Museum
ColBase（https://colbase.nich.go.jp/collection_items/tnm/TA-504?locale=ja）

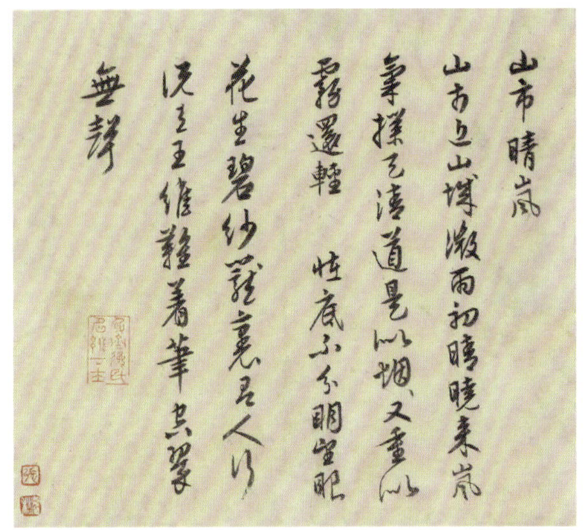

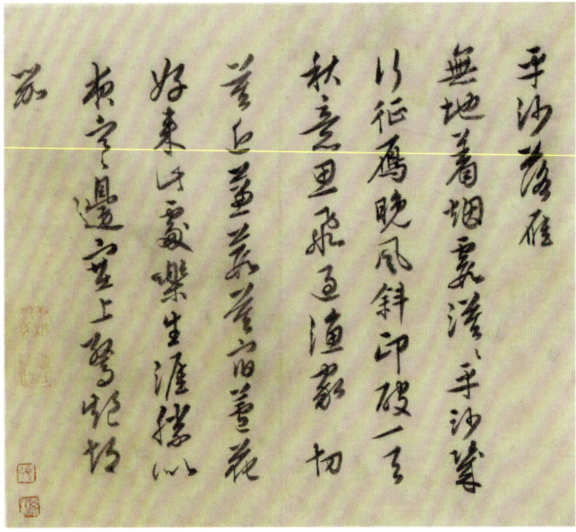

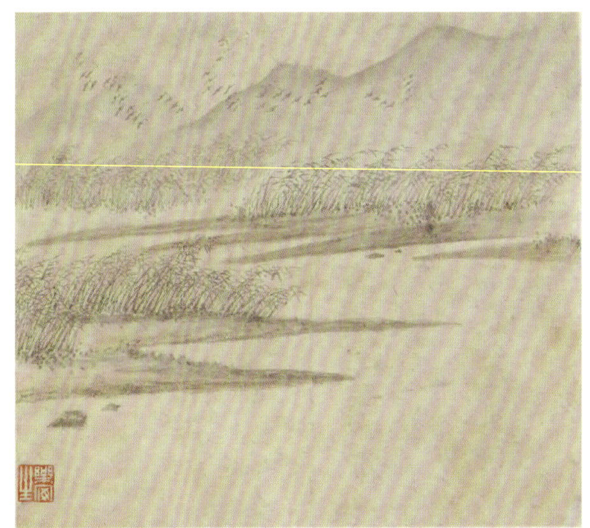

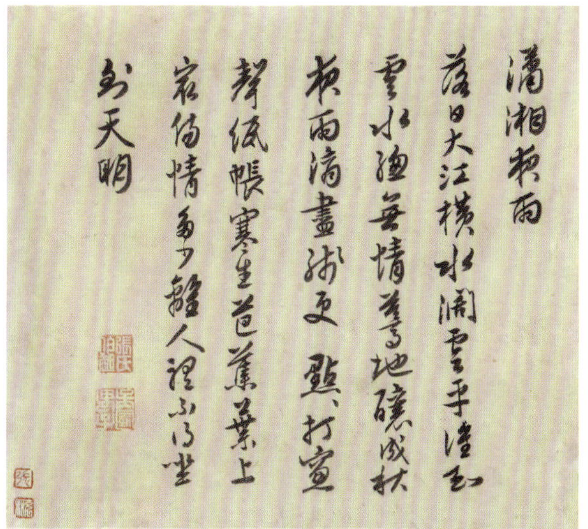

202. 潇湘八景图

明
孙枝、张凤翼
纸本设色
册页
每开：纵37.6、横37.3厘米
耶鲁大学艺术博物馆

Eight Views of Xiao and Xiang

Ming dynasty (1368–1644)
Sun Zhi and Zhang Fengyi
Ink and color on paper
Album leaf
H×W(each leaf) : 37.6×37.3 cm
The Yale University Art Gallery
Leonard C. Hanna, Jr., Class of 1913, Fund

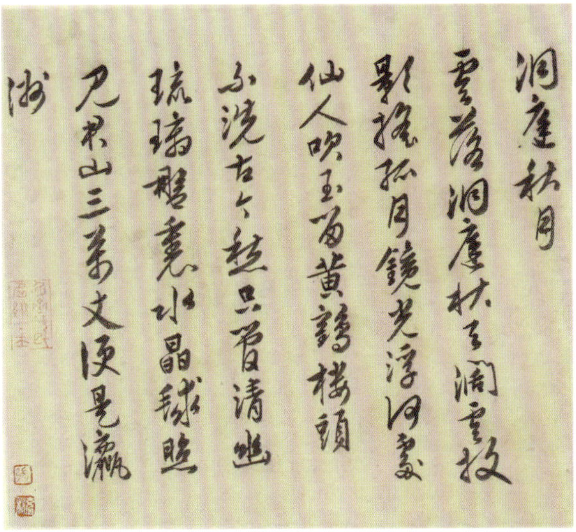
洞庭秋月

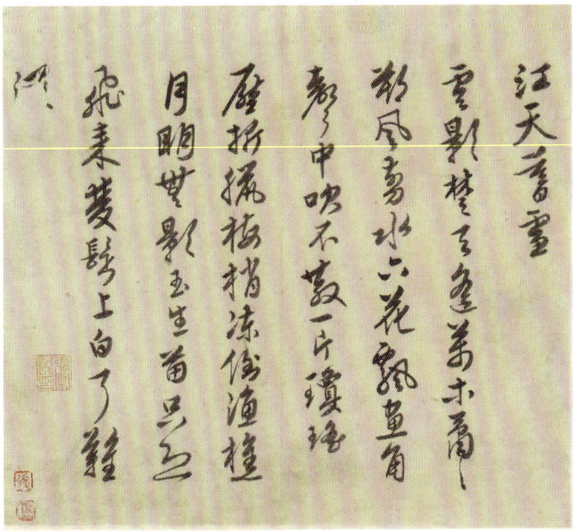
江天暮雪

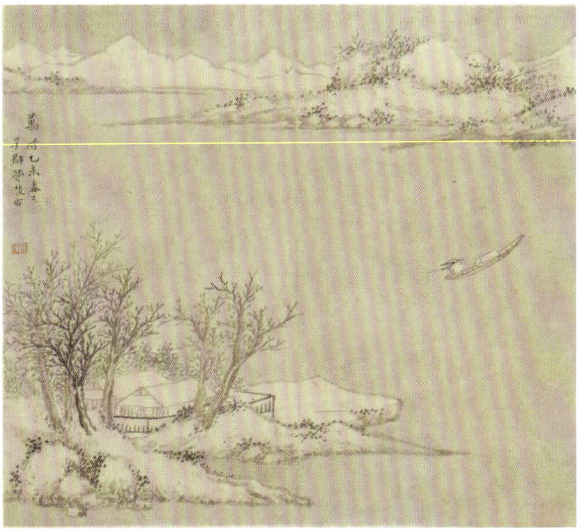

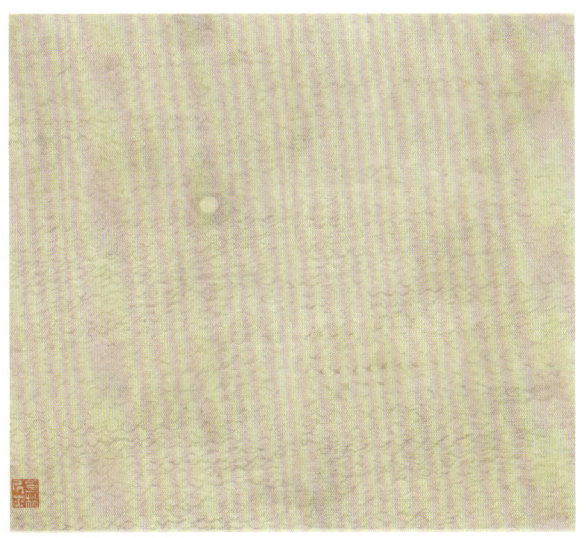

漁村夕照

江上白雲寒流水漾漾漁
翁家住蘆花灘[illegible]
[illegible]前[illegible]無路[illegible]
落日半啣山[illegible]
溪紅斜照[illegible]圖罷收
[illegible]編竿沽一醉[illegible]

[illegible]

烟寺曉鐘

煙鎖梵王宮[illegible]鐘一聲
[illegible]月[illegible]中惱殺啼鳥
尚不住[illegible]西風[illegible]耳
[illegible]何事匆匆少年
催促白頭翁今古相催鼓
不盡此恨無[illegible]

203. 寒山访友图

明崇祯四年（公元1631年）
刘原起
纸本设色
立轴
纵127.6、横59.7厘米
耶鲁大学艺术博物馆

Returning with Crane on Snowy River

Ming dynasty (1368–1644), dated 1631
Liu Yuanqi
Ink and color on paper
Hanging scroll
H×W : 127.6×59.7 cm
The Yale University Art Gallery
Gift of Wango H.C. Weng

204. 高山图

明隆庆三年（公元1569年）
侯懋功
纸本设色
立轴
纵118.4、横27.9厘米
大都会艺术博物馆

High Mountains

Ming dynasty (1368–1644), dated 1569
Hou Maogong
Ink and color on paper
Hanging scroll
H×W : 118.4×27.9 cm
The Metropolitan Museum of Art
Bequest of John M. Crawford Jr., 1988

205. 寒林钟馗图

Zhong Kui, Demon Queller

明万历三十八年（公元1610年）
陈焕
纸本设色
立轴
纵130、横29.3厘米
耶鲁大学艺术博物馆

Ming dynasty (1368–1644), dated 1610
Chen Huan
Ink and color on paper
Hanging scroll
H×W : 130×29.3 cm
The Yale University Art Gallery
Gift of Wango H.C. Weng

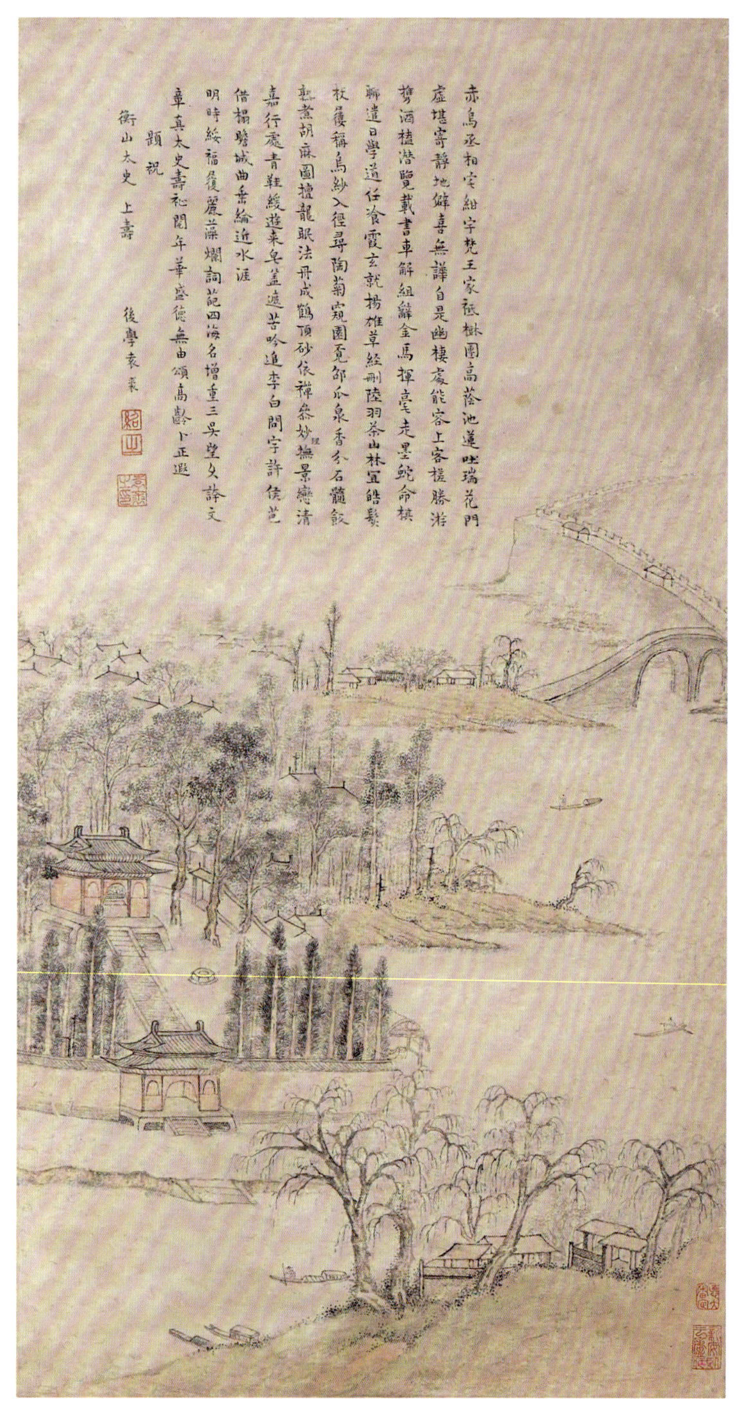

206. 为文徵明作山水图

明

袁裘

纸本设色

立轴

纵67.31、横35.88厘米

明尼阿波利斯美术馆

Suzhou Temple Garden

Ming dynasty (1368–1644)

Yuan Qiu

Ink and color on paper

Hanging scroll

H×W : 67.31×35.88 cm

The Minneapolis Institute of Art

Gift of Joan Wurtele

207. 抑斋曾叔祖八十五龄寿像

Portrait of Artist's Great-granduncle Yizhai at Age of Eighty-five

明
阮祖德
绢本设色
立轴
纵156.8、横96.2厘米
大都会艺术博物馆

Ming dynasty (1368–1644)
Ruan Zude
Ink and color on silk
Hanging scroll
H×W : 156.8×96.2 cm
The Metropolitan Museum of Art
Seymour Fund, 1959

208. 老妇像

明
阮祖德
绢本设色
立轴
纵156.8、横96.2厘米
大都会艺术博物馆

Portrait of Old Lady

Ming dynasty (1368–1644)
Ruan Zude
Ink and color on silk
Hanging scroll
H×W : 156.8×96.2 cm
The Metropolitan Museum of Art
Seymour Fund, 1959

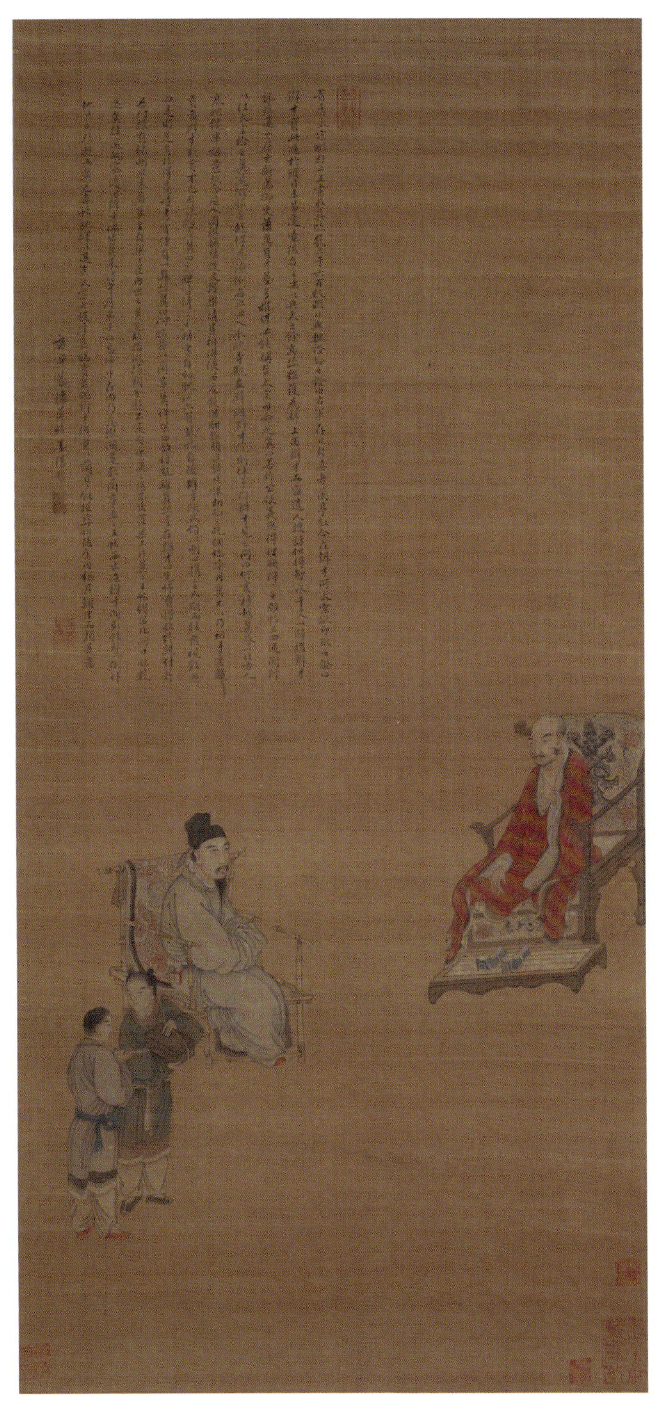

209. 萧翼赚兰亭图

Xiao Yi Obtaining Lanting Preface from Biancai

明
姜隐
绢本设色
立轴
纵108、横47.6厘米
耶鲁大学艺术博物馆

Ming dynasty (1368–1644)
Jiang Yin
Ink and color on silk
Hanging scroll
H×W : 108×47.6 cm
The Yale University Art Gallery
Leonard C. Hanna, Jr., Class of 1913, Fund

210. 仿北苑山水图

Landscape After Dong Yuan

明清之际
陆克正
纸本水墨
册页
纵16.5、横50.8厘米
大都会艺术博物馆

Late Ming to early Qing dynasty
Lu Kezheng
Ink on paper
Album leaf
H×W : 16.5×50.8 cm
The Metropolitan Museum of Art
John Stewart Kennedy Fund, 1913

211. 牧牛图

明
秦舜友
绢本设色
册页
纵26.1、横27.9厘米
弗利尔美术馆

Boy on Water Buffalo

Ming dynasty (1368–1644)
Qin Shunyou
Ink and color on silk
Album leaf
H×W : 26.1×27.9 cm
The Freer Gallery of Art
Gift of Charles Lang Freer

辛巳春二月張翀畫

212. 田家春斗图

明崇祯十四年（公元1641年）
张翀
绢本水墨
手卷
纵20.32、横177.8厘米
印第安纳波利斯艺术博物馆

Farmers Fighting in Springtime

Ming dynasty (1368–1644), dated 1641
Zhang Chong
Ink on silk
Handscroll
H×W : 20.32×177.8 cm
The Indianapolis Museum of Art
Gift of Francine and Roger Hurwitz

213. 花鸟图

明
张翀
纸本水墨
册页
纵16.5、横48.9厘米
大都会艺术博物馆

Bird on Flowering Branch

Ming dynasty (1368–1644)
Zhang Chong
Ink on paper
Album leaf
H×W : 16.5×48.9 cm
The Metropolitan Museum of Art
John Stewart Kennedy Fund, 1913

214. 杏花双禽图

明
周之冕
绢本设色
立轴
纵133.1、横58.6厘米
耶鲁大学艺术博物馆

Birds, Rocks and Flowering Prunus

Ming dynasty (1368–1644)
Zhou Zhimian
Ink and color on silk
Hanging scroll
H×W : 133.1×58.6 cm
The Yale University Art Gallery
Gift of Edward Lee Cave in memory of
Edward Francis Cave

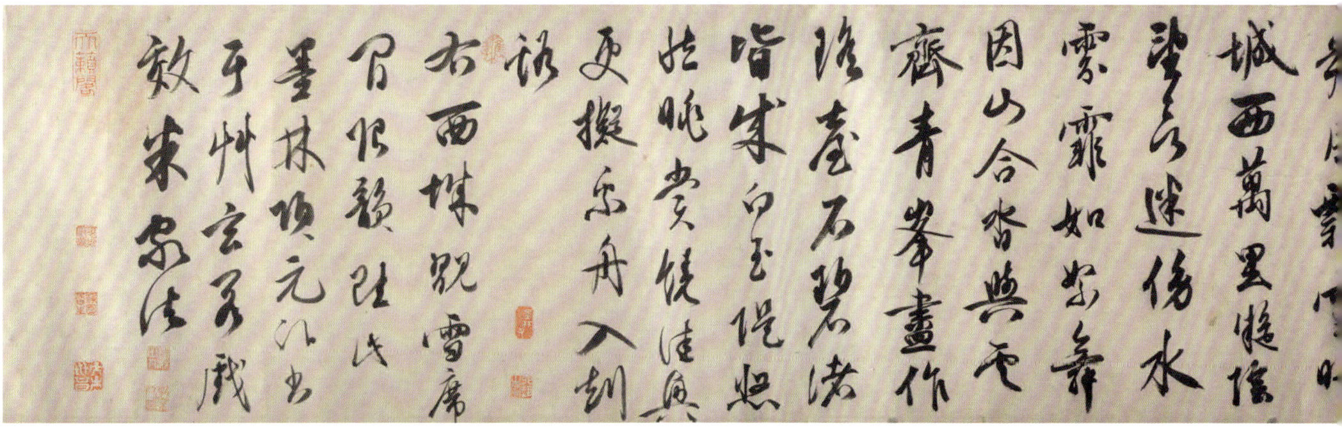

215. 秋江图

明万历六年（公元1578年）
（传）项元汴
纸本水墨
手卷
纵30.2、横92.7厘米
大都会艺术博物馆

River Landscape

Ming dynasty (1368–1644), dated 1578
Attributed to Xiang Yuanbian
Ink on paper
Handscroll
H×W : 30.2×92.7 cm
The Metropolitan Museum of Art
Bequest of John M. Crawford Jr., 1988

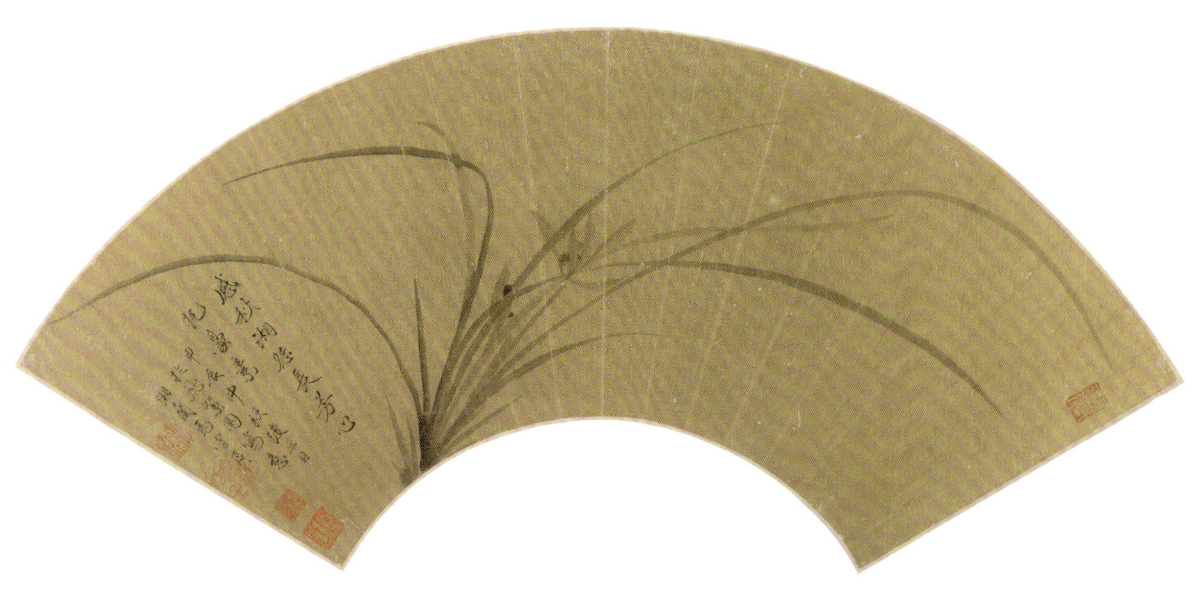

216. 墨兰图

明万历三十二年（公元1604年）
马守真
纸本水墨
册页
纵16.5、横51厘米
耶鲁大学艺术博物馆

Orchids

Ming dynasty (1368–1644), dated 1604
Ma Shouzhen
Ink on paper
Album leaf
H×W : 16.5×51 cm
The Yale University Art Gallery
Purchased with a gift from the B. D. G. Leviton Foundation and with the Stephen Carlton Clark, B.A. 1903, Fund

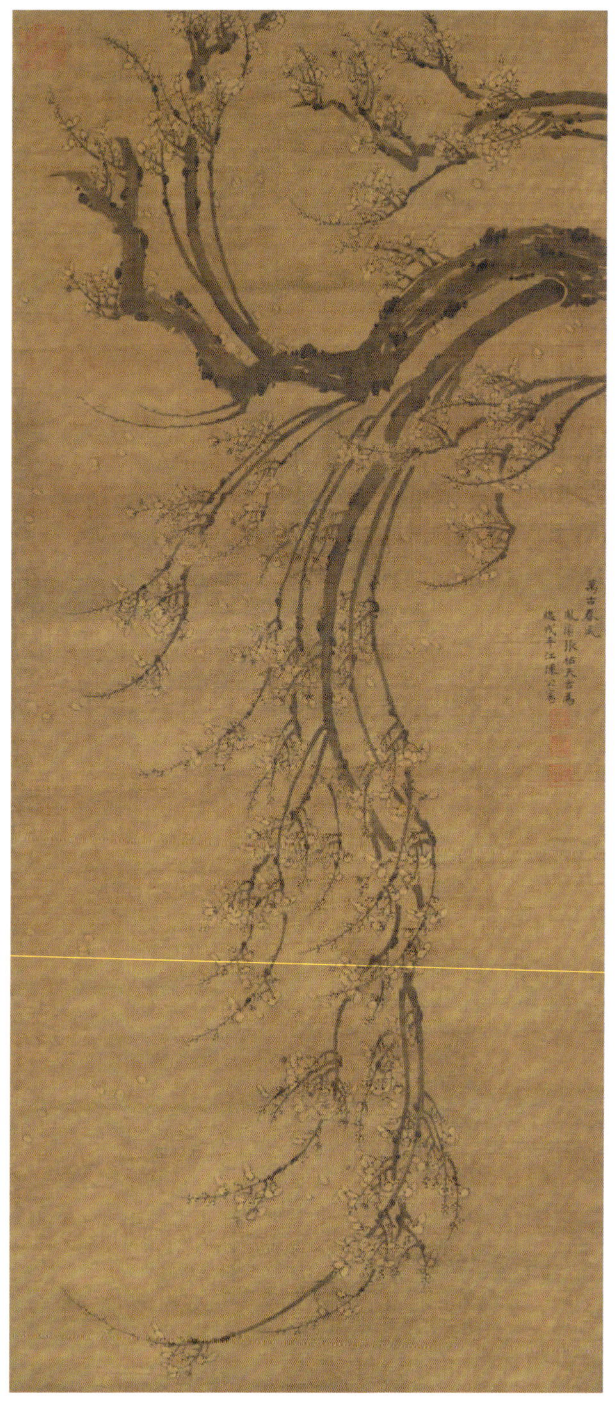

217. 万古春风图

明
张祐
绢本水墨
立轴
纵156.8、横69.9厘米
大都会艺术博物馆

Spring Breeze of Myriad Pasts

Ming dynasty (1368–1644)
Zhang You
Ink on silk
Hanging scroll
H×W : 156.8×69.9 cm
The Metropolitan Museum of Art
Edward Elliott Family Collection, Purchase,
The Dillon Fund Gift, 1981

218. 千山雪霁图

明万历二十一年（公元1593年）
宋旭
绢本设色
立轴
纵133.1、横58.6厘米
耶鲁大学艺术博物馆

Thousand Peaks After Snowfall

Ming dynasty (1368–1644), dated 1593
Song Xu
Ink and color on silk
Hanging scroll
H×W : 133.1×58.6 cm
The Yale University Art Gallery
Gift of Karen Wang in honor of Professor Shen C. Y. Fu

219. 山水图

明万历三十二年（公元1604年）
宋旭
绢本设色
立轴
纵163、横75.6厘米
波士顿美术博物馆

Landscape

Ming dynasty (1368–1644), dated 1604
Song Xu
Ink and color on silk
Hanging scroll
H×W : 163×75.6 cm
The Museum of Fine Arts, Boston
Keith McLeod Fund 1973.173

鳳皇山

新塘

烏瞻山

220. 湖州十八景图

明
宋旭
绢本设色
册页
每开：纵26.4、横28.4厘米
克利夫兰美术馆

Eighteen Views of Huzhou Yutai Peak

Ming dynasty (1368–1644)
Song Xu
Ink and color on silk
Album leaf
H×W(each leaf) : 26.4×28.4 cm
The Cleveland Museum of Art
The Severance and Greta Millikin Purchase Fund 1998.78

沈長山

合溪市

仙頂

歸雲菴

玉臺峰

洞山

福山院

黃龍洞

小梅

碧浪湖

221. 仿黄公望山水图

明万历九年（公元1581年）
莫是龙
纸本设色
立轴
纵119.1、横41厘米
大都会艺术博物馆

Landscape After Huang Gongwang

Ming dynasty (1368–1644), dated 1581
Mo Shilong
Ink and color on paper
Hanging scroll
H×W : 119.1×41 cm
The Metropolitan Museum of Art
Gift of Ernest Erickson Foundation, 1985

222. 荷塘花鸟图

明崇祯十六年（公元1643年）
陈嘉言
纸本水墨
立轴
纵120、横51.9厘米
耶鲁大学艺术博物馆

Birds by Lotus Pond

Ming dynasty (1368–1644), dated 1643
Chen Jiayan
Ink on paper
Hanging scroll
H×W : 120×51.9 cm
The Yale University Art Gallery
Gift of Nelson I. Wu in honor of the memory of Hartley Simpson (1900–1967), historian, educator, and friend, Dean of the Graduate School, Yale University,1956–1961

223. 竹石水仙图

Bamboo, Rock, and Narcissus

清顺治九年（公元1652年）
陈嘉言
纸本水墨
立轴
纵80、横43.5厘米
金贝尔艺术博物馆

Late Ming to early Qing dynasty, dated 1652
Chen Jiayan
Ink on paper
Hanging scroll
H×W : 80×43.5 cm
The Kimbell Art Museum
Kimbell Art Museum, Fort Worth, Texas. AP 1984. 20

224. 菊石图

清康熙二年（公元1663年）
陈嘉言
纸本水墨
册页
纵16.5、横51.9厘米
耶鲁大学艺术博物馆

Chrysanthemums and Rock

Late Ming to early Qing dynasty, dated 1663
Chen Jiayan
Ink on paper
Album leaf
H×W : 16.5×51.9 cm
The Yale University Art Gallery
Gift of Edward Lee Cave in memory of Edward Francis Cave, by exchange

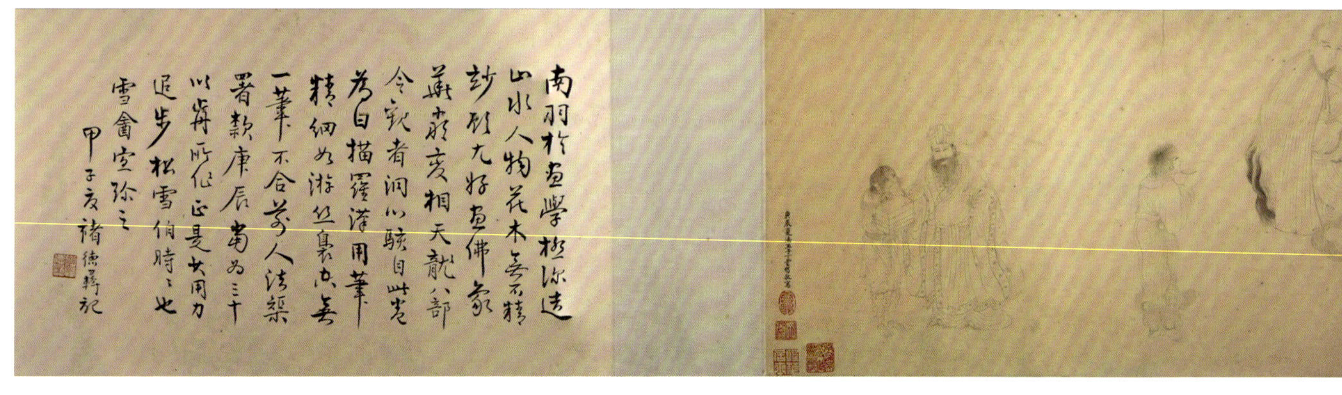
南羽於畫學極深造
山水人物花木無不精
妙所尤好畫佛家
菩薩變相天龍八部
令觀者洞心駭目此卷
為白描羅漢用筆
精細如游絲裊空無
一筆不合古人法
署款庚辰蓋為三十
甲子夏褚德彝記

225. 白描罗汉图

明万历八年（公元1580年）
丁云鹏
纸本水墨
手卷
纵26、横341.5厘米
普林斯顿大学美术馆

Baimiao Arhats

Ming dynasty (1368–1644), dated 1580
Ding Yunpeng
Ink on paper
Handscroll
H×W : 26×341.5 cm
The Princeton University Art Museum
Museum purchase, Fowler McCormick, Class of 1921, Fund, and gift of Lloyd E. Cotsen, Class of 1950, in honor of Wen C. Fong, Class of 1951 and Graduate School Class of 1958

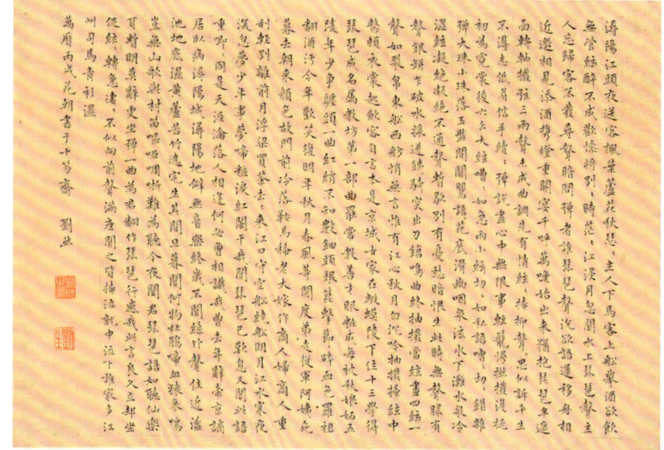

226. 浔阳送客图

Song of Lute

明万历十三年（公元1585年）
丁云鹏
纸本设色
立轴
纵141.3、横46厘米
大都会艺术博物馆

Ming dynasty (1368–1644), dated 1585
Ding Yunpeng
Ink and color on paper
Hanging scroll
H×W : 141.3×46 cm
The Metropolitan Museum of Art
John Stewart Kennedy Fund, 1913

227. 天都晓日图

Morning Sun over Heavenly Citadel Peak

明万历四十二年（公元1614年）
丁云鹏
纸本设色
立轴
纵212.7、横55.4厘米
克利夫兰美术馆

Ming dynasty (1368–1644), dated 1614
Ding Yunpeng
Ink and color on paper
Hanging scroll
H×W : 212.7×55.4 cm
The Cleveland Museum of Art
Andrew R. and Martha Holden Jennings Fund
1965.28

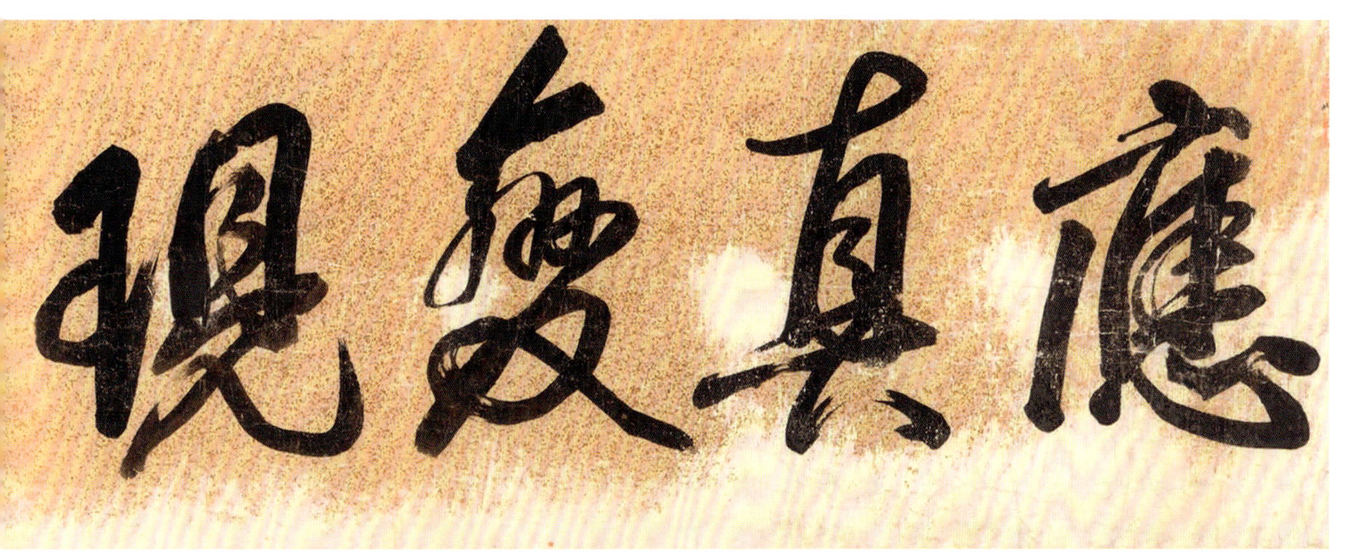
應真變現

228. 十六罗汉图

明万历十九年（公元1591年）
吴彬
纸本设色
手卷
纵32.1、横415.4厘米
大都会艺术博物馆

Sixteen Luohans

Ming dynasty (1368–1644), dated 1591
Wu Bin
Ink and color on paper
Handscroll
H×W : 32.1×415.4 cm
The Metropolitan Museum of Art
Edward Elliott Family Collection, Gift of Douglas Dillon, 1986

依般若波羅蜜多故心
罣礙無罣礙故無有恐
怖遠離顛倒夢想究
竟涅槃三世諸佛依般
若波羅蜜多故得阿耨
多羅三藐三菩提故知
般若波羅蜜多是大神
呪是大明呪是無上呪
是無等等呪能除一切苦
真實不虛故說般若波
羅蜜多呪即說呪曰揭
諦揭諦波羅揭諦波
羅僧揭諦菩提薩婆
訶

睦庵湯睿尹盥手書

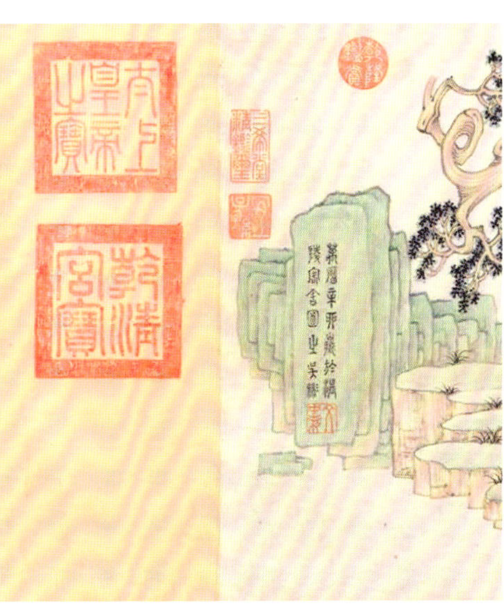

般若波羅蜜多心經
觀自在菩薩行深般若
波羅蜜多時照見五蘊皆
空度一切苦厄舍利子色
不異空空不異色色即是
空空即是色受想行識
亦復如是舍利子是諸法
空相不生不滅不垢不淨
不增不減故空中無色
無受想行識無眼耳
鼻舌身意無色聲香
味觸法無眼界乃至無意
識界無無明亦無無明盡
乃至無老死亦無老死盡

229. 翠壁丹枫图

Green Cliff with Red Maples

明万历三十一年（公元1603年）
吴彬
纸本设色
册页
纵16.2、横47.6厘米
大都会艺术博物馆

Ming dynasty (1368–1644), dated 1603
Wu Bin
Ink and color on paper
Album leaf
H×W : 16.2×47.6 cm
The Metropolitan Museum of Art
John Stewart Kennedy Fund, 1913

230. 五百罗汉图

明
吴彬
纸本设色
手卷
纵37.7、横2347厘米
克利夫兰美术馆

Five Hundred Arhats

Ming dynasty (1368–1644)
Wu Bin
Ink and color on paper
Handscroll
H×W : 37.7×2347 cm
The Cleveland Museum of Art
John L. Severance Fund 1971.16

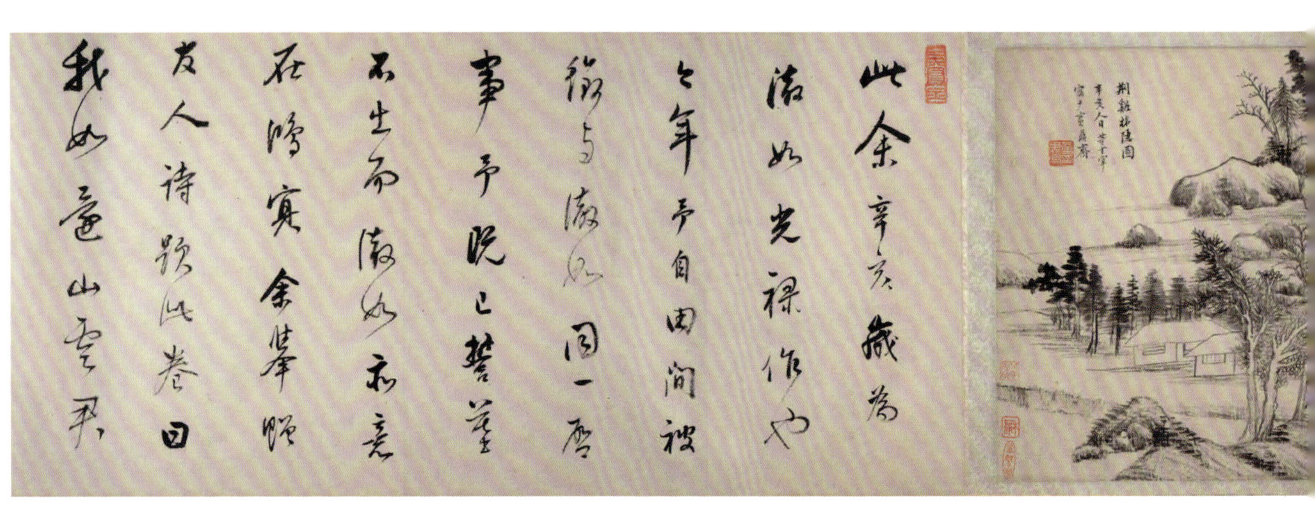

中歲以鯁直為權門要人陳洽所逐
光祿之席未煖遂為湖州司李玄宰叔
見惡斯人者不覺同病相憐訪余雲棲
棲頭貽以二卷一應既合後蒲泉居玄
宰者未出山余時為小筆亦當之誌
彭蠡拂衣而後此圖並第先識其令而
後山中日月正長白首先為載之應船召
字誌遂堅不為弋者所慕又豈待招而
後隱哉

丁巳夏至日長蟄散人吳正志識

沈景倩野獲編載僧慧秀
能詩為吳徵如比部所厚築
菴陽羨以居之後徵如轉江右
兵使慧秀竟棄瓢笠稱山人
未幾慧秀叛而徵如之長君
洪亮以勸誘慧秀還俗犯佛
戒故遭冥譴其事甚怪殆不
足論余嘗見宜興志知徵如為
吳中名宿家世最盛其雲起
樓至今尚在也

丁丑二月同龢謹記

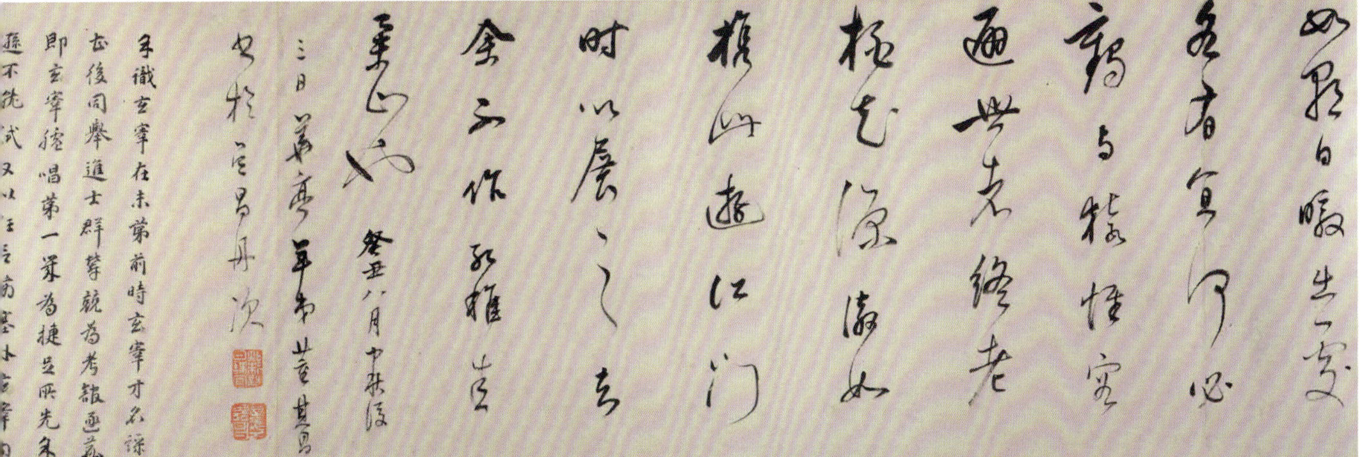

231. 荆溪招隐图

明万历三十九年（公元1611年）
董其昌
纸本水墨
手卷
纵26、横92.6厘米
大都会艺术博物馆

Invitation to Reclusion at Jingxi

Ming dynasty (1368–1644), dated 1611
Dong Qichang
Ink on paper
Handscroll
H×W : 26×92.6 cm
The Metropolitan Museum of Art
Gift of Mr. and Mrs. Wan-go H. C. Weng, 1990

232. 青弁图

明万历四十五年（公元1617年）
董其昌
纸本水墨
立轴
纵225、横67.6厘米
克利夫兰美术馆

Qingbian

Ming dynasty (1368–1644), dated 1617
Dong Qichang
Ink on paper
Hanging scroll
H×W: 225×67.6 cm
The Cleveland Museum of Art
Leonard C. Hanna, Jr. Fund 1980.10

233. 仿倪瓒松亭秋色图

Pavilion Under Pine Trees in Autumn After Ni Zan

明天启元年（公元1621年）
董其昌
纸本水墨
立轴
纵138.5、横53.7厘米
波士顿美术博物馆

Ming dynasty (1368–1644), dated 1621
Dong Qichang
Ink on paper
Hanging scroll
H×W : 138.5×53.7 cm
The Museum of Fine Arts, Boston
Gift of the Wan-go H. C. Weng Collection and the Weng family, in honor of Weng Tonghe 2018.2911

234. 山水图

Steep Mountains and Silent Waters

明崇祯五年（公元1632年）
董其昌
纸本水墨
立轴
纵102.5、横30.3厘米
金贝尔艺术博物馆

Ming dynasty (1368–1644), dated 1632
Dong Qichang
Ink on paper
Hanging scroll
H×W : 102.5×30.3 cm
The Kimbell Art Museum
Kimbell Art Museum, Fort Worth, Texas. AP 1980. 02

巖居高士圖
玄宰

235. 仿古山水图

明崇祯十一年（公元1638年）
董其昌
纸本水墨
册页
每开：纵24.4、横16厘米
大都会艺术博物馆

Landscapes After Old Masters

Ming dynasty (1368–1644), dated 1638
Dong Qichang
Ink on paper
Album leaf
H×W(each leaf) : 24.4×16 cm
The Metropolitan Museum of Art
Edward Elliott Family Collection, Gift of Douglas Dillon, 1986

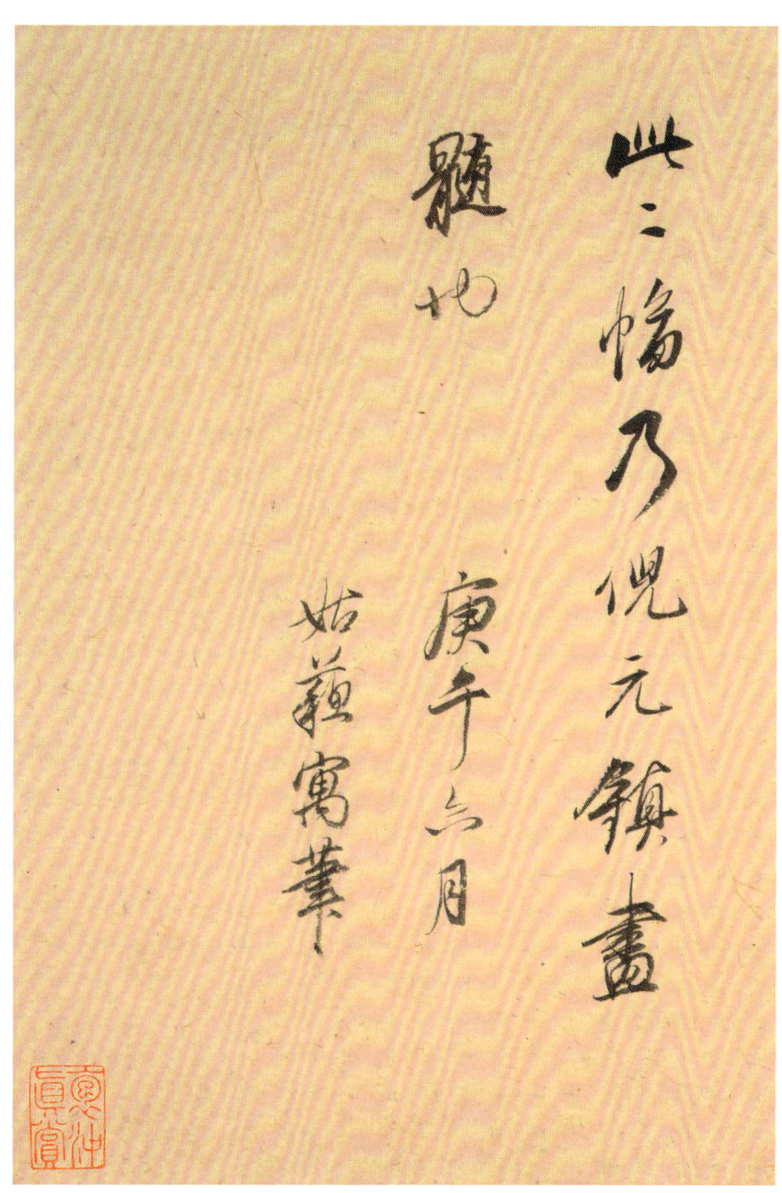
此二幅乃倪元鎮畫
髓也
庚午六月
姑蘇寓筆

巖居高士啚
玄宰

江山蕭寺
倣巨然筆
玄宰

炊煙連宿靄
隱〻見松亭〻
中有靜者單
讀淨名經
玄宰

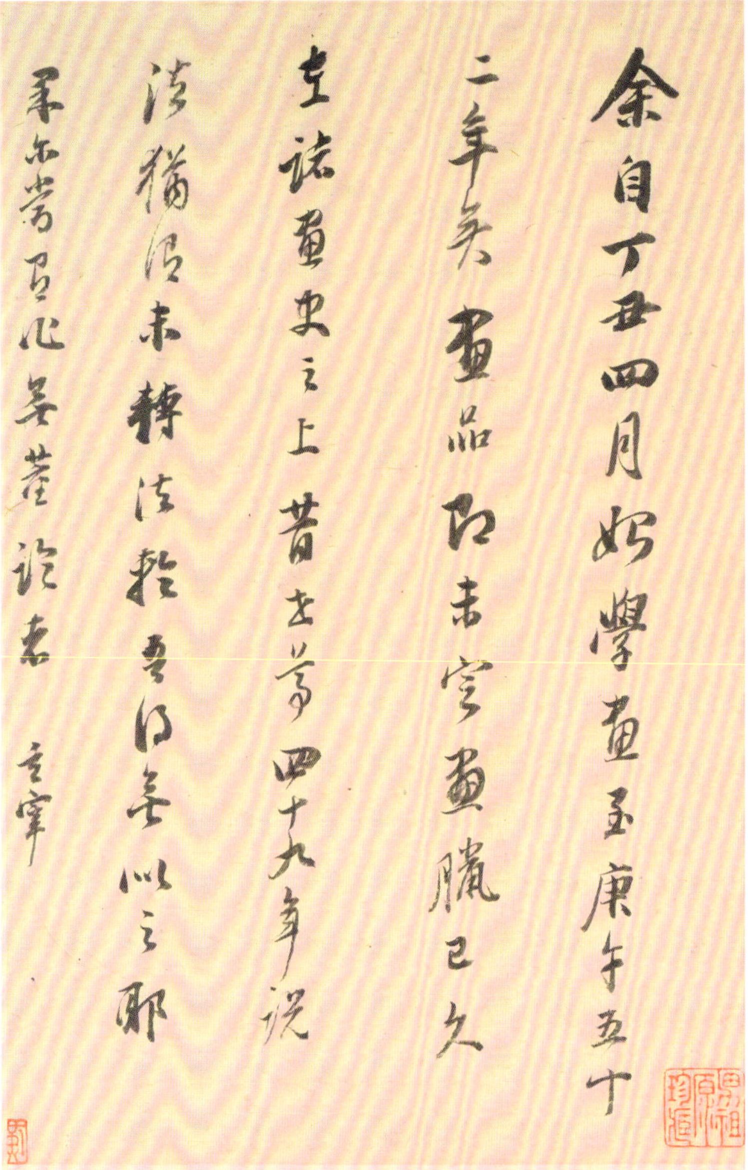

余自丁丑四月始學畫至庚午五十
二年矣畫品雖未定畫臘已久
在諸畫史之上昔世尊四十九年說
法猶得未轉法輪吾何吝以之耶
畢竟當具心眼甚讀者　玄宰

庚午九月九日寫此
八景　七十六翁

此香光晚年極得意筆其蒼厚渾古之氣直逼北宗諸賢何止倪黃而已然非真知畫理如綠扶者不能賞之 文治記

丙辰除夕前三日吾友張兄秋塘携香光畫冊見過一展閱知巳丑歲侍 先君子見於城北李氏者也李氏先以儒術起家富收藏 先君子挈恭訪之時值秋杪庭前古楓一本橫斜夭矯猶着餘花主人供茗花下論古款洽家後出二冊相賞一即是冊一為祝書小楷黃庭紙墨甚精後有董文敏歸文休二跋而董冊闌尤為汪文同堂所賞汪名應鶴号雲墻精鑒別 屈指今昔忽忽廿又七年矣香光畫冊忽來吾所回憶疇曩光景歷歷見畫如見 先君子披圖靜諦時也秋塘曰審是冊合歸君遂贖得而謹為之跋

嘉慶元年嘉平月廿八日謹庭陸恭剪燭書

236. 建溪山水图

明
董其昌
纸本设色
立轴
纵125.3、横47.1厘米
耶鲁大学艺术博物馆

Reminiscence of Jian River

Ming dynasty (1368–1644)
Dong Qichang
Ink and color on paper
Hanging scroll
H×W : 125.3×47.1 cm
The Yale University Art Gallery
Leonard C. Hanna, Jr., Class of 1913, Fund; Mrs. Paul Moore Fund; and Anonymous Oriental Purchase Fund

237. 仿董源溪山樾馆图

Shaded Dwellings Among Streams and Mountains After Dong Yuan

明
董其昌
纸本水墨
立轴
纵158.4、横72.1厘米
大都会艺术博物馆

Ming dynasty (1368–1644)
Dong Qichang
Ink on paper
Hanging scroll
H×W : 158.4×72.1 cm
The Metropolitan Museum of Art
Gift of Douglas Dillon, 1979

238. 仿巨然山水图

明
董其昌
绫本水墨
手卷
纵24.2、横245.1厘米
波士顿美术博物馆

Landscape After Ju Ran and Calligraphy

Ming dynasty (1368–1644)
Dong Qichang
Ink on satin
Handscroll
H×W : 24.2×245.1 cm
The Museum of Fine Arts, Boston
Gift of the Wan-go H. C. Weng Collection and the Weng family, in memory of Virginia Dzung Weng
2010.1031

仿巨然
筆意

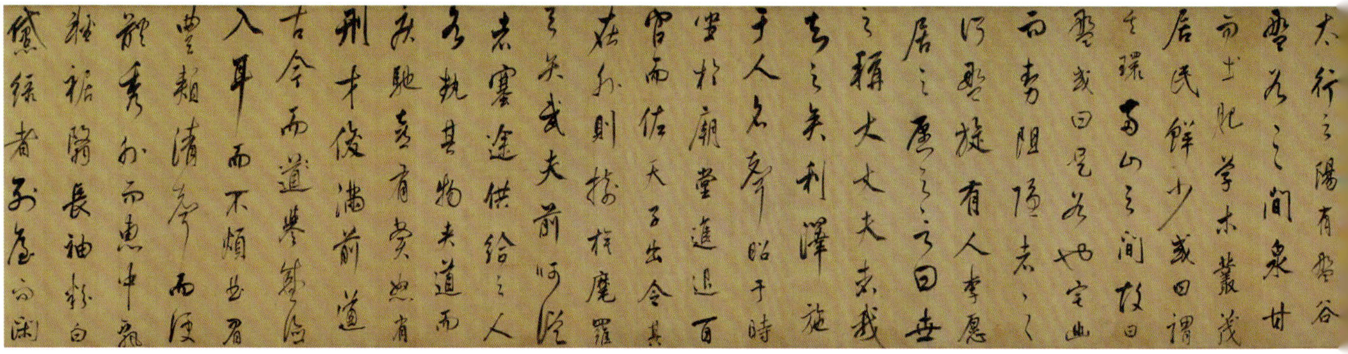

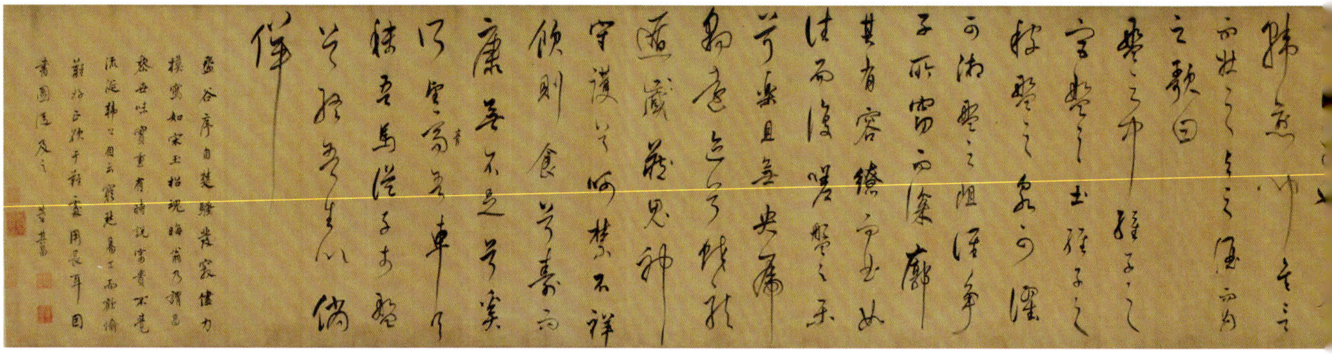

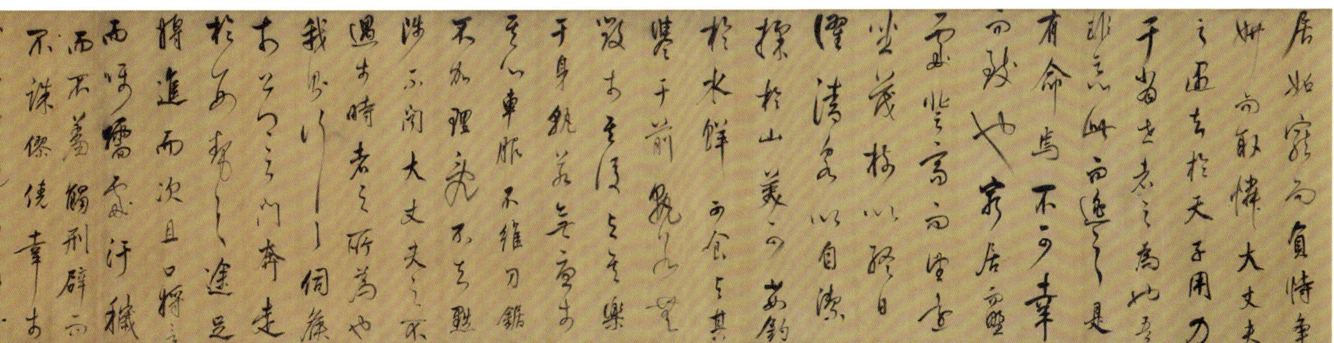

239. 盘谷序书画合璧图

Calligraphy and Painting Based on Han Yu's Preface to Li Yuan Retreats to Pangu

明
董其昌
纸本设色
手卷
纵40.6厘米
大阪市立美术馆

Ming dynasty (1368–1644)
Dong Qichang
Ink and color on paper
Handscroll
W : 40.6 cm
The Osaka City Museum of Fine Arts

董文敏每遇高黄鏡面箋書畫尤為入神
此卷改希伐用之字蹟渾然兼有相鮮之
印至於筆法圖秀真接倪黃豈文沈所可
同日而語也
康熙庚午中秋後一日吳興燈下弟初華題於粉膺 把竹翁高士奇

康熙甲戌九月廿三日趣裝北上舟過吳閶
漫堂先生載酒相餞得話數年別緒因以
平日所藏書畫請為鑒定漫堂先生未有
文敏畫卷遂留此志別茲卷得有所歸可
成他日佳話時立冬之四日天寒清霜樹
紅黃与卷中筆墨互相映帶并之漫堂先
生一詩紀之附以不朽 江村高士奇

昭代鑒賞誰第一棠邨之後推江邨五年蒼湖暫休沐
摩挲卷軸窮朝昏昨歲寄我銷夏錄雲烟過眼
賓第令年春 君北赴 閱書畫船泊吾江濱
相見不暇作寒暄珊瑚之網出異珍含題玉躞謂未有
傾囊倒篋縱横陳卷舒寧翁眠乘手攜有數封
不欠仲三日颯然落之康者時大叫忽主賓寫太山
圖表尖帖無上妙迹欣相執楓楊祖府真不在華
亭書處詩更捫烟江 烟江疊嶂圖 秋齋兩喜移氣韻生
動真天人秋齋長不滿三尺高髮表紙先如銀一重
一捲師造化一樹一石總點塵逆來詩證昌画理莫寫
朝日相鮮新鼓云古人不我見大難心折定九原朱
印燦燦尤奇目點綴更足重與璠先生好我卑忒
贈題識數語情彌款欲留不得拍命屠包裹脫
我衣巾要剖長歌記揚事把辭良愧奪止貧
歸來重展帽屢鼓缺得先射苦塲根苦冷猶君
退山寄句猶不了則真錄入卷尾是寄所此詩共
畫爭千春 西陂教稿 宋犖

元明兩代文敏後有宗伯前王孫王孫獨
攬舊雲秀書精畫妙驚鉄塵宗伯去之三百
載風流文采宣後身浚析已歷文祀浏緻染
况擁倪黄觀此卷自題微于大江山齋景澄
鮮特高勝鏡面紙三尺深深平遠闊無根沙
草微施□細逶清沦浅渚荒江濱断岸無人
帶景約隔嗟攀藏烟部雲豪秀潤叢樹活
筆墨神盡無纖痕我不能畫識畫理明窗幽
晴融心神誰欲快者高唐事大內鑒賞精绝
論漫堂先生尔得之珍比珣玗琪瑤琨示客
相汁寒具油裹將鄭幡白純巾還來吟羊徒
紅薜沈欲與畫争千春斯語非□壺瓷許果
然此詩此畫争千春
昆陵邵長蘅奉和

240. 江山秋霁图

明
董其昌
纸本水墨
手卷
纵38.4、横136.8厘米
克利夫兰美术馆

River and Mountains on Clear Autumn Day

Ming dynasty (1368–1644)
Dong Qichang
Ink on paper
Handscroll
H×W : 38.4×136.8 cm
The Cleveland Museum of Art
Purchase from the J. H. Wade Fund 1959.46

憭淡秋光濯
眼新大癡昨
夜入精神思
翁亦豈自誇
筆叫絕奚妨
愜古人
乾隆戊寅御題

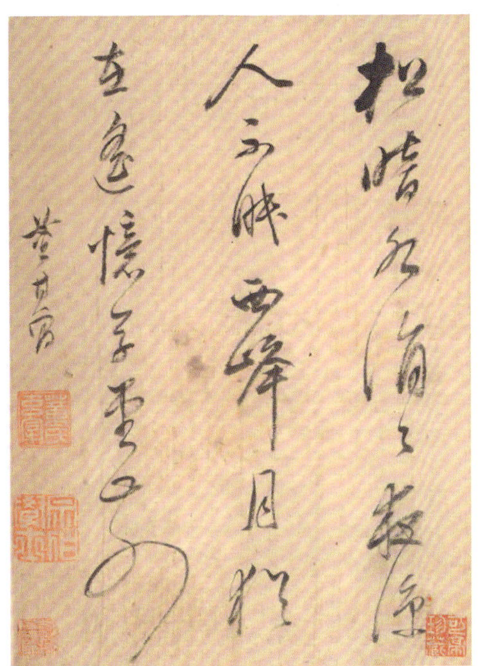

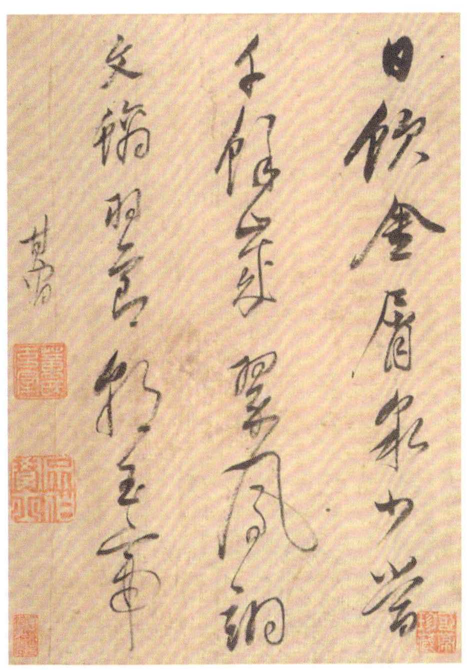

241. 仿古山水图

明
董其昌
纸本设色
册页
每开：纵32.1、横23.2厘米
大都会艺术博物馆

Landscapes and Poems After Masters

Ming dynasty (1368–1644)
Dong Qichang
Ink and color on paper
Album leaf
H×W(each leaf) : 32.1×23.2 cm
The Metropolitan Museum of Art
Gift of Mr. and Mrs. Wan-go H. C. Weng, 1989

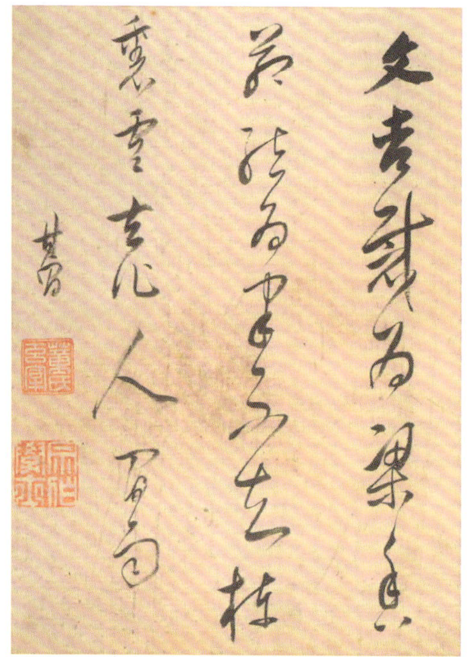

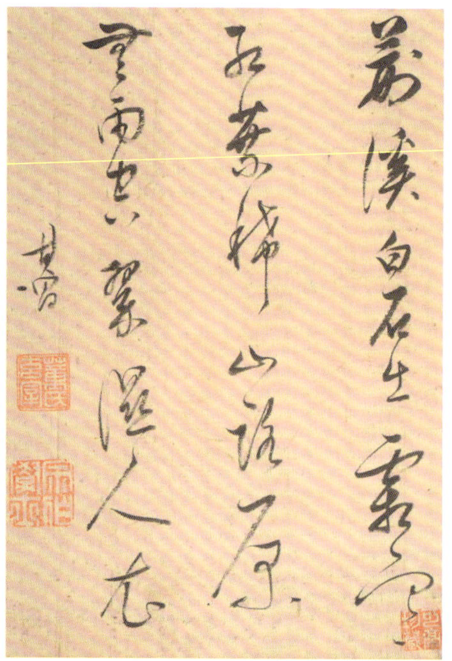

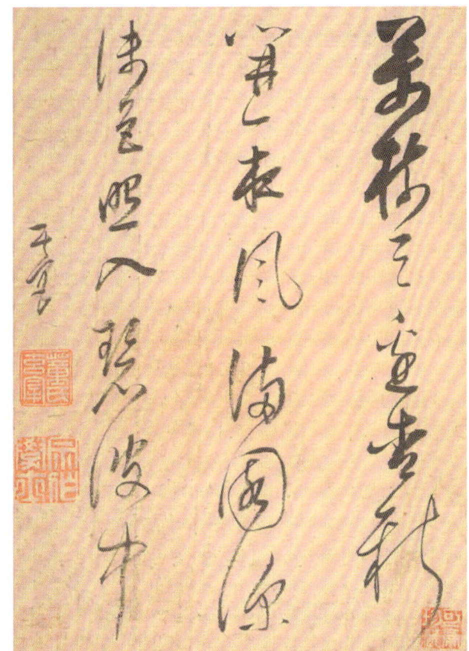

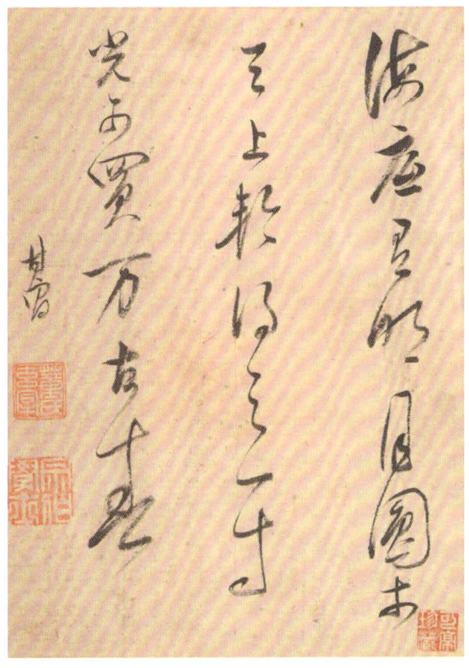

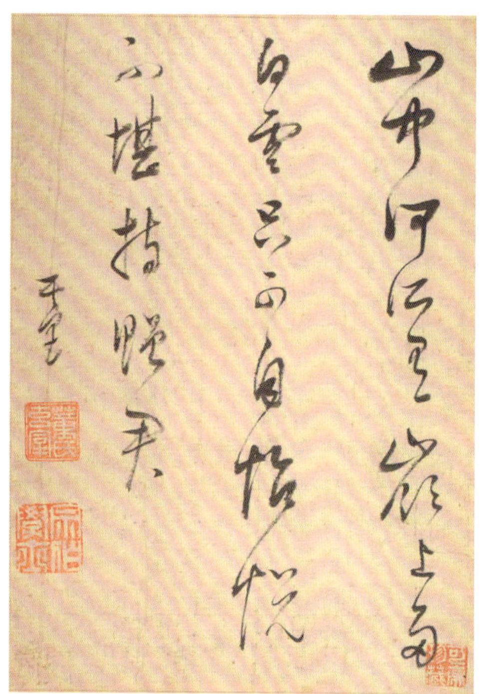

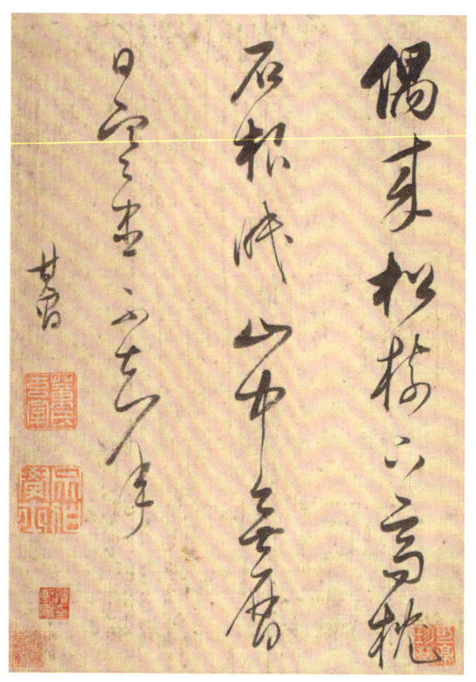

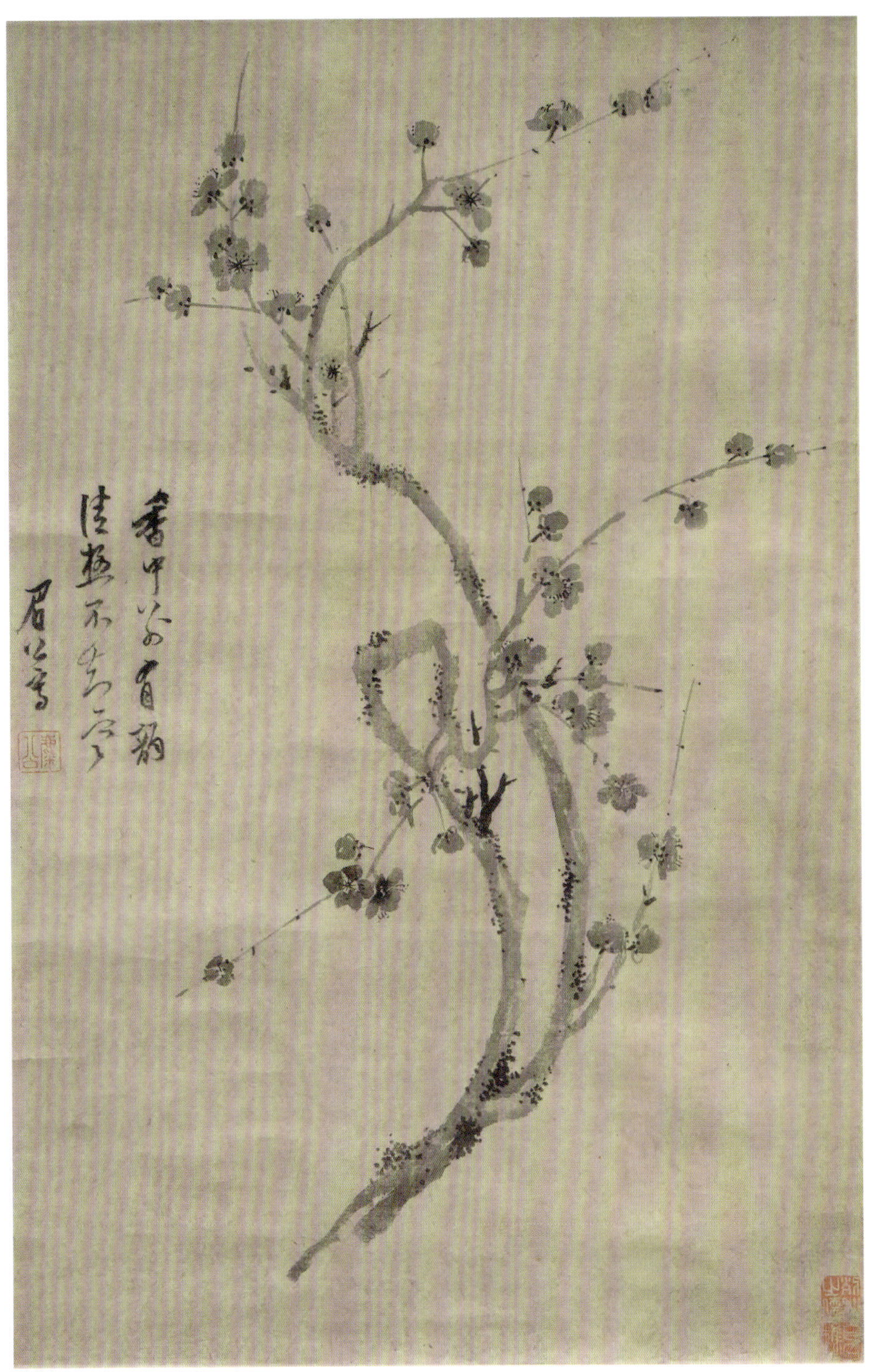

242. 墨梅图

明
陈继儒
纸本水墨
立轴
纵74.3、横48.6厘米
耶鲁大学艺术博物馆

Cut Branch of Blossoming Plum

Ming dynasty (1368–1644)
Chen Jiru
Ink on paper
Hanging scroll
H×W : 74.3×48.6 cm
The Yale University Art Gallery
S. Sidney Kahn, B.A. 1959, Fund

畫家六法以氣韻為貴然氣韻生乎法非以法求氣韻也猶之文字之妙生乎法非以法求妙也大家氣韻出于自然凡家則求之其他并不知求矣李成王蒙黃公望王詵倪元鎮吳仲圭筆俱法董巨其虛實避就傾向深淺各自成家而氣韻之自然者出

香山

春山競渡圖本趙大年作也大家名令穰宋宗室擁富勢裘馬而獨
有筆墨之嗜惜未能遍遊名山大川其筆意尚少蒼龍入海氣色耳
昔人謂其胷次再加萬卷書便可通乎造化蓋画法通于讀書其語
非始于董宗伯也然吾每見大年出筆頗類儒氣豈右將軍不識字而
行軍暗与古合者欤令人亦有名讀書者而作畫反師匠人則其先天
之品不足道耳　惲向自題

243. 仿古山水图

明清之际
恽向
纸本设色
册页
每开：纵26、横15.2厘米
大都会艺术博物馆

Landscapes After Old Masters

Late Ming to early Qing dynasty
Yun Xiang
Ink and color on paper
Album leaf
H×W(each leaf) : 26×15.2 cm
The Metropolitan Museum of Art
Purchase, Douglas Dillon Gift, 1977

王右軍書如龍跳天門虎臥鳳闕歷代寶之永以為訓蓋非筆之正鋒不足以尚此畫家筆必竟自古法中右軍書也須觀其一筆中皆有元氣

道生記于泗上之玻璃泉亭腳下

求其似處，又求其不似處，無所取之形，其遠也。明則不深，無所取之形，其蒙蒙然也。深則不明，無所取之形，其歷歷然也。直則不曲，無所取之形，其直而曲也。促則不濶，無所取之形，其促而濶也。

于前篇似近而更遠，只擅出一筆中亦有遠處，學者知之，使古人出地可焉。

暑中湯華道人

惠崇蘆寒滅没人鳥欲藏之意每看筆
令愁我始欲愁
香山向

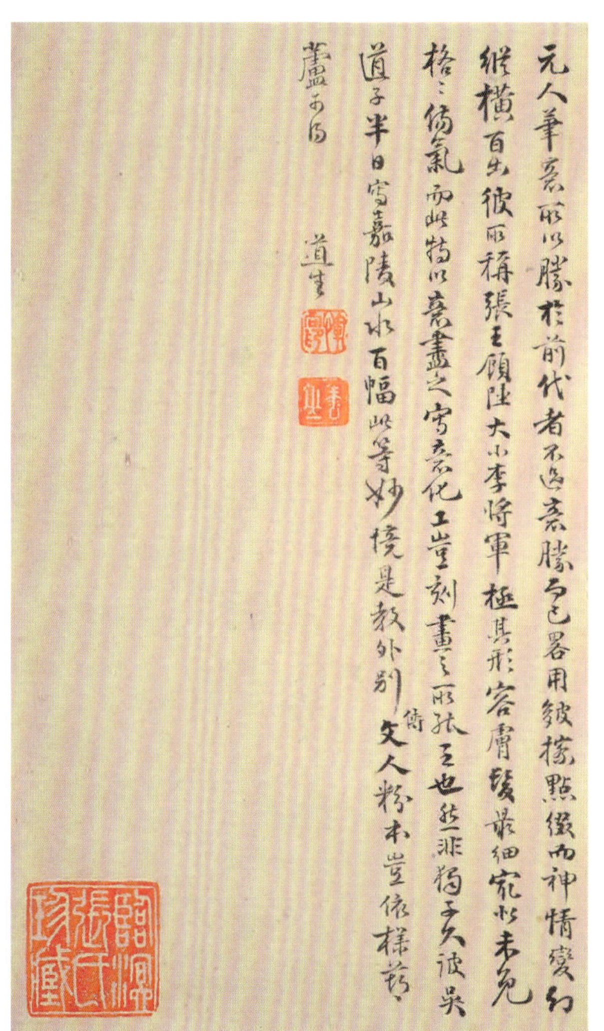

此沒骨山水圖其法出自僧繇僧繇多窮工極變且大米亦極變而多存其意所謂莖草者大約畫不盡圖勝於畫也 道生

禪家南北二宗唐時始分畫家之南北二宗亦唐時始分但其人非南北耳北宗則李思訓父子著色山水流傳而為宋之趙幹趙伯駒伯驌以至馬夏諸人南宗則王摩詰始用渲淡一變鉤斫之法其傳為張璪荊關郭忠恕董巨米家父子以至元之四大家亦如六祖之後馬駒雲門臨濟兒孫之盛而北宗微矣摩詰所謂雲峯石跡迥出天機筆意縱橫參乎造化者真[illegible][illegible]耳夏日訪藥老寫此一冊并題發笑 寅年治弟惲著

帶筆帶墨無筆無墨乃有筆有墨此非狐禪語也
是廼謂之神氣凡倪迂設色畫法多不出奇無間以
奇意出之如娘子軍整暇忽出而乳丈夫子如擒曹縱李
號氣色振壁上觀為儒宗品外奪冕

道生父書於鎮陽水上

此篇近中之遠不於遠取遠者凡逸品多不變化吾欲臨其丈六金身遂多變化姑作三種以俟悟人着眼語云急須着眼看僊人莫看僊人手中扇

香山

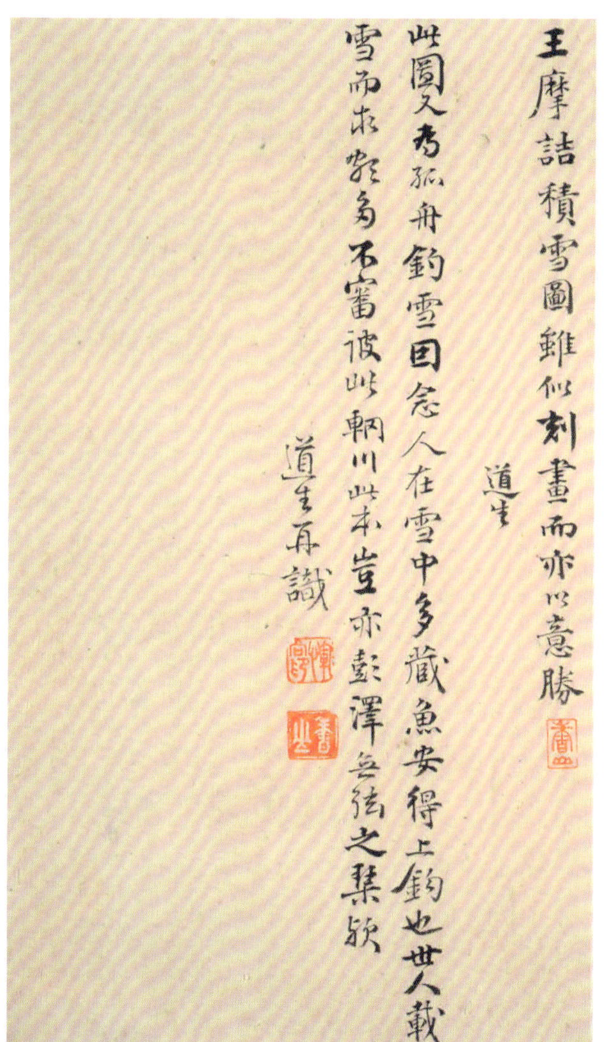
王摩詰積雪圖雖似刻畫而亦以意勝
道生
此圖又為孤舟釣雪因念人在雪中多藏魚安得上鉤也世人載
雪而求繪爲不啻彼此輞川此本豈亦彭澤無弦之琹歟
道生再識

邵瓜疇雲山平遠圖

244. 云山平远图

Expansive Views of Clouds and Mountains

明崇祯十三年（公元1640年）
邵弥
纸本水墨
手卷
纵26、横781.7厘米
大阪市立美术馆

Ming dynasty (1368–1644), dated 1640
Shao Mi
Ink on paper
Handscroll
H×W : 26×781.7 cm
The Osaka City Museum of Fine Arts

245. 仿文徵明山水图

明崇祯十三年（公元1640年）
邵弥
纸本设色
册页
纵16.5、横47.6厘米
大都会艺术博物馆

Landscape After Wen Zhengming

Ming dynasty (1368–1644), dated 1640
Shao Mi
Ink and color on paper
Album leaf
H×W : 16.5×47.6 cm
The Metropolitan Museum of Art
John Stewart Kennedy Fund, 1913

246. 濯足图

明崇祯二年（公元1629年）
陈祼
纸本设色
册页
纵16.5、横49.8厘米
大都会艺术博物馆

Recluse Washing His Feet in Stream

Ming dynasty (1368–1644), dated 1629
Chen Guan
Ink and color on paper
Album leaf
H×W : 16.5×49.8 cm
The Metropolitan Museum of Art
John Stewart Kennedy Fund, 1913

247. 抚琴图

明崇祯五年（公元1632年）
程嘉燧
纸本水墨
册页
纵22.3、横51厘米
芝加哥艺术博物馆

Scholar Playing Qin

Ming dynasty (1368–1644), dated 1632
Cheng Jiasui
Ink on paper
Album leaf
H×W : 22.3×51 cm
The Art Institute of Chicago
Mr. and Mrs. Samuel M. Nickerson Endowment Fund

248. 乔松磐石图

明崇祯十二年（公元1639年）
程嘉燧
纸本水墨
立轴
纵158.43、横63.18厘米
明尼阿波利斯美术馆

Lofty Pines and Great Rock

Ming dynasty (1368–1644), dated 1639
Cheng Jiasui
Ink on paper
Hanging scroll
H×W : 158.43×63.18 cm
The Minneapolis Institute of Art
Gift of Ruth and Bruce Dayton

巖下有幽人
松圓程嘉燧製

一葉浮水面
松圓老人程嘉燧

249. 山水二帧

明
程嘉燧
纸本设色
册页
每开：纵35.6、横35.6厘米
大都会艺术博物馆

Two Landscapes

Ming dynasty (1368–1644)
Cheng Jiasui
Ink and color on paper
Alumb leaf
H×W(each leaf) : 35.6×35.6 cm
The Metropolitan Museum of Art
Gift of Florence and Herbert Irving, 2015

250. 竹院逢僧图

Scholar and Monk in Zhuyuan Buddhist Cloister

明
赵左
纸本设色
立轴
纵67.9、横31.2厘米
大阪市立美术馆

Ming dynasty (1368–1644)
Zhao Zuo
Ink and color on paper
Hanging scroll
H×W : 67.9×31.2 cm
The Osaka City Museum of Fine Arts

251. 溪山无尽图

Streams and Mountains Without End

明
赵左
纸本设色
手卷
纵24.4、横631.5厘米
大都会艺术博物馆

Ming dynasty (1368–1644)
Zhao Zuo
Ink and color on paper
Handscroll
H×W : 24.4×631.5 cm
The Metropolitan Museum of Art
Purchase, The Dillon Fund Gift, 1976

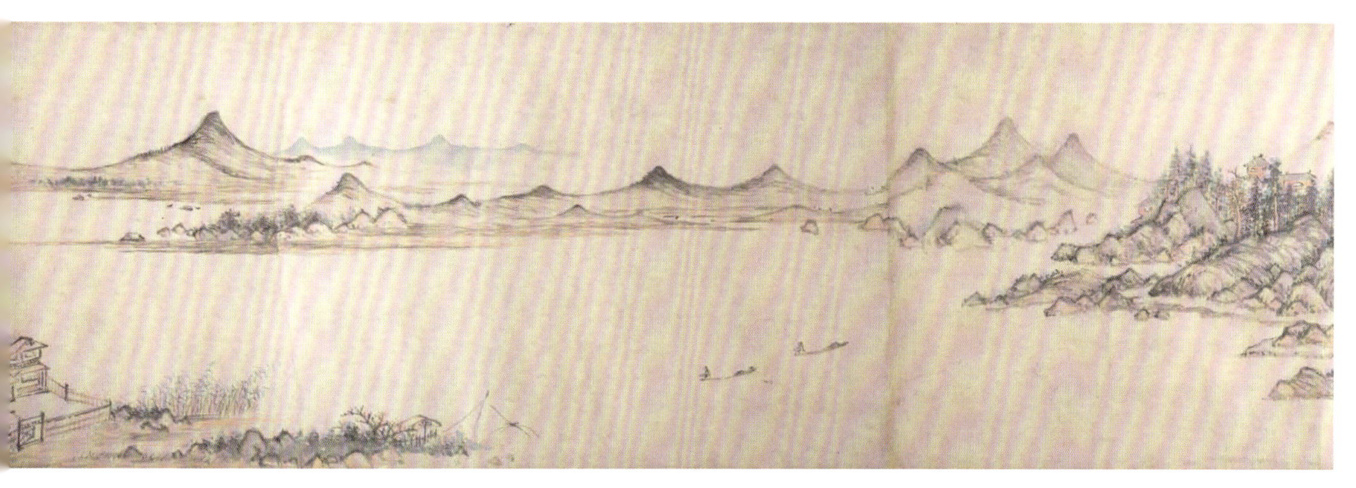

252. 墨竹图

明万历四十一年（公元1613年）
归昌世
纸本水墨
立轴
纵109、横29.5厘米
普林斯顿大学美术馆

Bamboo

Ming dynasty (1368–1644), dated 1613
Gui Changshi
Ink on paper
Hanging scroll
H×W : 109×29.5 cm
The Princeton University Art Museum
Gift of DuBois Schanck Morris, Class of 1893

253. 疏林小景图

明万历四十一年（公元1613年）
李流芳
纸本设色
册页
纵18.4、横55.6厘米
大都会艺术博物馆

Landscape

Ming dynasty (1368–1644), dated 1613
Li Liufang
Ink and color on paper
Album leaf
H×W : 18.4×55.6 cm
The Metropolitan Museum of Art
John Stewart Kennedy Fund, 1913

乙丑春日
作溪山邨
舍
李流芳

254. 溪山村舍图

明天启五年（公元1625年）
李流芳
纸本水墨
扇面
纵18.5、横55厘米
集美博物馆

Landscape

Ming dynasty (1368–1644), dated 1625
Li Liufang
Ink on paper
Fan
H×W : 18.5×55 cm
The Guimet Museum

255. 踈林远山图

明崇祯元年（公元1628年）
李流芳
纸本水墨
立轴
纵114.3、横40.3厘米
克利夫兰美术馆

Thin Forest and Distant Mountains

Ming dynasty (1368–1644), dated 1628
Li Liufang
Ink on paper
Hanging scroll
H×W : 114.3×40.3 cm
The Cleveland Museum of Art
John L. Severance Fund 1953.630

256. 秋窗读易图

明崇祯七年（公元1634年）
卞文瑜
纸本水墨
手卷
纵26、横108厘米
大都会艺术博物馆

Mountain and Stream in Autumn

Ming dynasty (1368–1644), dated 1634
Bian Wenyu
Ink on paper
Handscroll
H×W : 26×108 cm
The Metropolitan Museum of Art
Bequest of John M. Crawford Jr., 1988

257. 仿古山水图

Landscapes After Old Masters

清顺治七年（公元1650年）
卞文瑜
纸本水墨
册页
纵25.5、横17.6厘米
弗利尔美术馆

Late Ming to early Qing dynasty, dated 1650
Bian Wenyu
Ink on paper
Album leaf
H×W : 25.5×17.6 cm
The Freer Gallery of Art
Transfer from the United States Customs Service, Department of the Treasury

258. 墨竹图

明
朱鹭
绫本水墨
立轴
纵227.3、横66厘米
耶鲁大学艺术博物馆

Bamboo

Ming dynasty (1368–1644)
Zhu Lu
Ink on satin
Hanging scroll
H×W : 227.3×66 cm
The Yale University Art Gallery
Gift of Edward Lee Cave in memory of Edward Francis Cave

259. 秋林远岫图

Distant Peaks beyond Autumn Grove

明崇祯四年（公元1631年）
杨文骢
绫本水墨
立轴
纵144.5、横55.8厘米
大阪市立美术馆

Ming dynasty (1368–1644), dated 1631
Yang Wencong
Ink on satin
Hanging scroll
H×W : 144.5×55.8 cm
The Osaka City Museum of Fine Arts

崇禎戊寅春二月 貴州楊文驄

260. 山水图

明崇祯十一年（公元1638年）
杨文骢
纸本设色
手卷
纵27、横280厘米
阿姆斯特丹国家博物馆

Landscape

Ming dynasty (1368–1644), dated 1638
Yang Wencong
Ink and color on paper
Handscroll
H×W : 27×280 cm
The Rijksmuseum
On loan from the Royal Asian Art Society in The Netherlands (purchase from the R.H. van Gulik collection, 1953)

261. 山水花鸟图

明崇祯十二年（公元1639年）
项圣谟
纸本设色
册页
每开：纵28.3、横22.5厘米
大都会艺术博物馆

Landscapes, Flowers and Birds

Ming dynasty (1368–1644), dated 1639
Xiang Shengmo
Ink and color on paper
Album leaf
H×W(each leaf) : 28.3×22.5 cm
The Metropolitan Museum of Art
Edward Elliott Family Collection, Purchase, The Dillon Fund Gift, 1981

余嘗往還苕霅之間
得此真趣欣然命筆
項孔彰記

千巖競秀
万壑争流

伯子逸

一片孤雲明雁影千尋立
壁壯秋濤自憐幾度滾
江客半世雄心夢也勞
項聖謨

巖棲思訪圖詠

262. 岩栖思访图

清顺治五年（公元1648年）
项圣谟
纸本水墨
手卷
纵30.5、横273厘米
克利夫兰美术馆

Meditative Visit to Mountain Retreat: In Picture and in Words

Late Ming to early Qing dynasty, dated 1648
Xiang Shengmo
Ink on paper
Handscroll
H×W : 30.5×273 cm
The Cleveland Museum of Art
Purchase from the J. H. Wade Fund 1962.42

甲午九月朔畫
項聖謨
吳子見而喜之
晴酣霜老秋何處紫到山嵐紅到樹西西寒鴉噪晚風無人指點斜陽路

263. 秋景图

Autumn Landscape

清顺治十一年（公元1654年）
项圣谟
纸本设色
册页
纵24.8、横33厘米
大都会艺术博物馆

Late Ming to early Qing dynasty, dated 1654
Xiang Shengmo
Ink and color on paper
Alumb leaf
H×W : 24.8×33 cm
The Metropolitan Museum of Art
Seymour Fund, 1964

264. 竹石梧桐图

明

项圣谟

绫本水墨

立轴

纵194、横51.5厘米

耶鲁大学艺术博物馆

Wutong Tree, Bamboo and Rock

Ming dynasty (1368–1644)

Xiang Shengmo

Ink on satin

Hanging scroll

H×W : 194×51.5 cm

The Yale University Art Gallery

B. D. G. Leviton Foundation and Wilson P. Foss, Jr., Funds

265. 山水图

River and Mountain Landscape

明
项圣谟
纸本水墨
立轴
纵54、横27厘米
芝加哥艺术博物馆

Ming dynasty (1368–1644)
Xiang Shengmo
Ink on paper
Hanging scroll
H×W : 54×27 cm
The Art Institute of Chicago
Kate S. Buckingham Endowment Fund

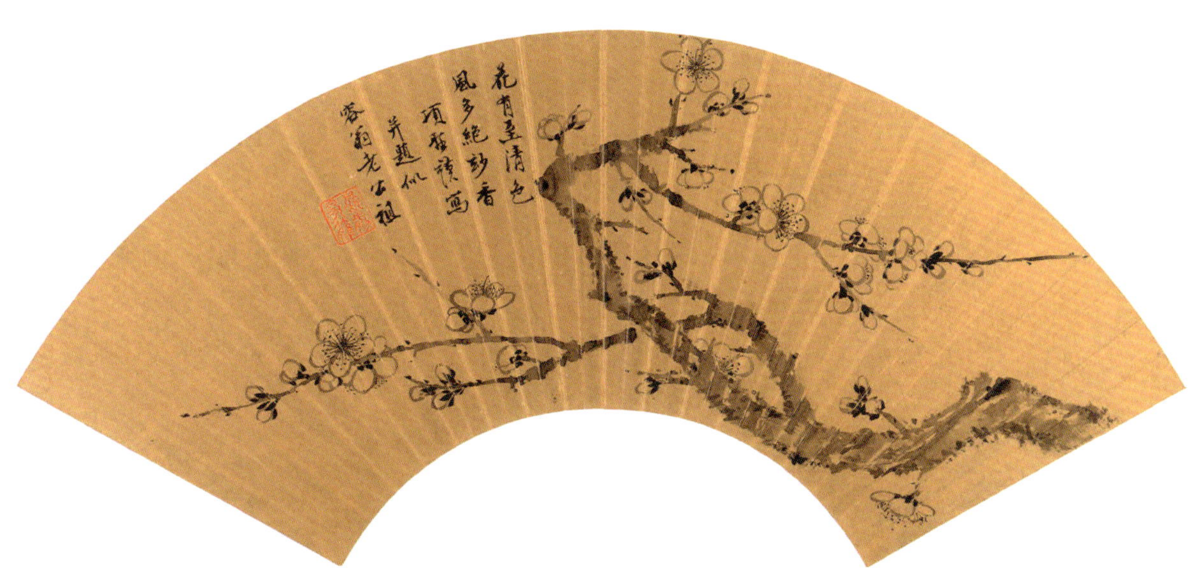

266. 梅花图

明
项圣谟
纸本水墨
册页
纵16.5、横50.8厘米
大都会艺术博物馆

Branch of Blossoming Plum

Ming dynasty (1368–1644)
Xiang Shengmo
Ink on paper
Album leaf
H×W : 16.5×50.8 cm
The Metropolitan Museum of Art
John Stewart Kennedy Fund, 1913

江山臥游圖 其九十
青溪道人
戊戌夏五
青溪道人與石谿為方外交其
筆墨亦有神似之處此卷臥
游圖純仿大癡用筆高簡絕去
十想不誣也

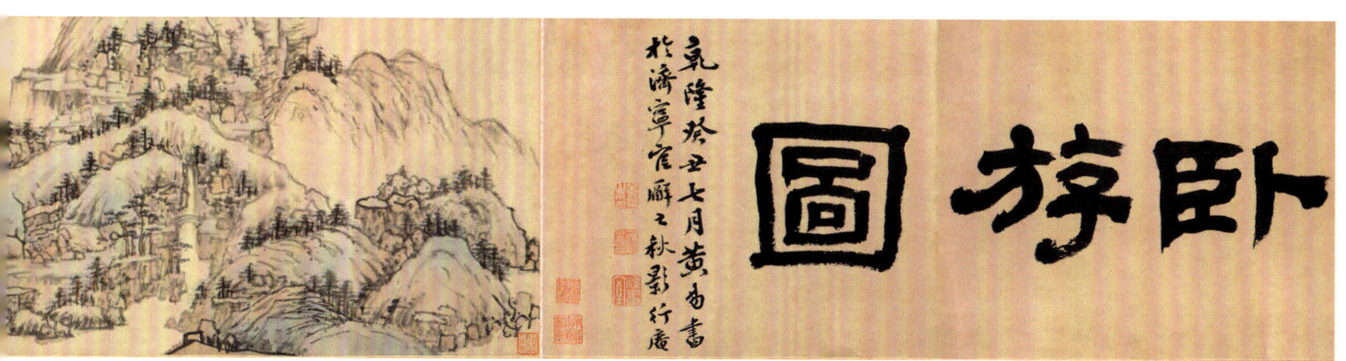
卧斿圖
乾隆癸丑七月黄易書
於濟寧官廨之秋影行庵

267. 江山卧游图

Dream Journey Among Rivers and Mountains

清顺治十五年（公元1658年）
程正揆
纸本设色
手卷
纵26、横344.2厘米
克利夫兰美术馆

Late Ming to early Qing dynasty, dated 1658
Cheng Zhengkui
Ink and color on paper
Handscroll
H×W : 26×344.2 cm
The Cleveland Museum of Art
Mr. and Mrs. William H. Marlatt Fund 1960.182

江山卧遊圖
青溪道人

268. 江山梦游图

清康熙元年（公元1662年）
程正揆
纸本设色
手卷
纵36.8、横921.7厘米
洛杉矶郡艺术博物馆

Dream Journey Among Rivers and Mountains

Late Ming to early Qing dynasty, dated 1662
Cheng Zhengkui
Ink and color on paper
Handscroll
H×W : 36.8×921.7 cm
The Los Angeles County Museum of Art
Far Eastern Art Council Fund (M.75.25)

269. 青谿卧游图	Dream Landscape
清康熙十三年（公元1674年）	Late Ming to early Qing dynasty, dated 1674
程正揆	Cheng Zhengkui
绢本设色	Ink and color on silk
手卷	Handscroll
纵23.2、横177.2厘米	H×W : 23.2×177.2 cm
大都会艺术博物馆	The Metropolitan Museum of Art
	Gift of Harry Lenart, 1955

270. 清溪入画图

明清之际
程正揆
纸本设色
立轴
纵110.2、横47.6厘米
耶鲁大学艺术博物馆

Reflections in Clear Stream

Late Ming to early Qing dynasty
Cheng Zhengkui
Ink and color on paper
Hanging scroll
H×W : 110.2×47.6 cm
The Yale University Art Gallery
Bankers Trust Company Foundation, Karen Y. Wang Fund, and Asian Discretionary Fund

王叔明溪橋翫月圖
顧原之光祿臨本有
青出于藍之致
董其昌

271. 临王蒙溪桥玩月图

Enjoying Moon: Landscape After Wang Meng

明崇祯元年（公元1628年）
顾懿德
纸本设色
立轴
纵154.9、横46.4厘米
大都会艺术博物馆

Ming dynasty (1368–1644), dated 1628
Gu Yide
Ink and color on paper
Hanging scroll
H×W : 154.9×46.4 cm
The Metropolitan Museum of Art
John Stewart Kennedy Fund, 1913

272. 延陵琴瀑图

明

顾见龙

绢本设色

手卷

纵28、横106.2厘米

科隆东亚艺术博物馆

Portrait of Wu Yihan

Ming dynasty (1368–1644)

Gu Jianlong

Ink and color on silk

Handscroll

H×W : 28×106.2 cm

Museum of East Asian Art, Cologne

Rheinisches Bildarchiv Köln, Mennicken, Marion, 04.02.2019

273. 仿关仝山溪待渡图

Waiting for Ferry After Guan Tong

明万历四十七年（公元1618年）
蒋蔼
绢本水墨
立轴
纵172.88、横84.93厘米
明尼阿波利斯美术馆

Ming dynasty (1368–1644), dated 1618
Jiang Ai
Ink on silk
Hanging scroll
H×W : 172.88×84.93 cm
The Minneapolis Institute of Art
Gift of Ruth and Bruce Dayton

274. 嵩山高图

明天启七年（公元1627年）
蓝瑛
绢本设色
立轴
纵193、横97.4厘米
波士顿美术博物馆

Lofty Mount Song

Ming dynasty (1368–1644), dated 1627
Lan Ying
Ink and color on silk
Hanging scroll
H×W : 193×97.4 cm
The Museum of Fine Arts, Boston
Julia Bradford Huntington James Fund

春江漁隱
壬申夏仲畫為
藍瑛

275. 春江渔隐图

Hermit-fisherman on Spring River

明崇祯五年（公元1632年）
蓝瑛
绢本设色
手卷
纵184.8、横90.8厘米
大都会艺术博物馆

Ming dynasty (1368–1644), dated 1632
Lan Ying
Ink and color on silk
Handscroll
H×W : 184.8×90.8 cm
The Metropolitan Museum of Art
Bequest of John M. Crawford Jr., 1988

276. 仿宋元山水图

Landscapes After Song and Yuan Masters

明崇祯十五年（公元1642年）
蓝瑛
纸本设色
册页
每开：纵31.6、横24.8厘米
大都会艺术博物馆

Ming dynasty (1368–1644), dated 1642
Lan Ying
Ink and color on paper
Album leaf
H×W(each leaf) : 31.6×24.8 cm
The Metropolitan Museum of Art
The Sackler Fund, 1970

趙令穰意似
二南社翁正之
藍溪

米南宮楚山清曉

擬大癡
江山勝覽
卷法以
二酉先生
鑒定

范華原畫法

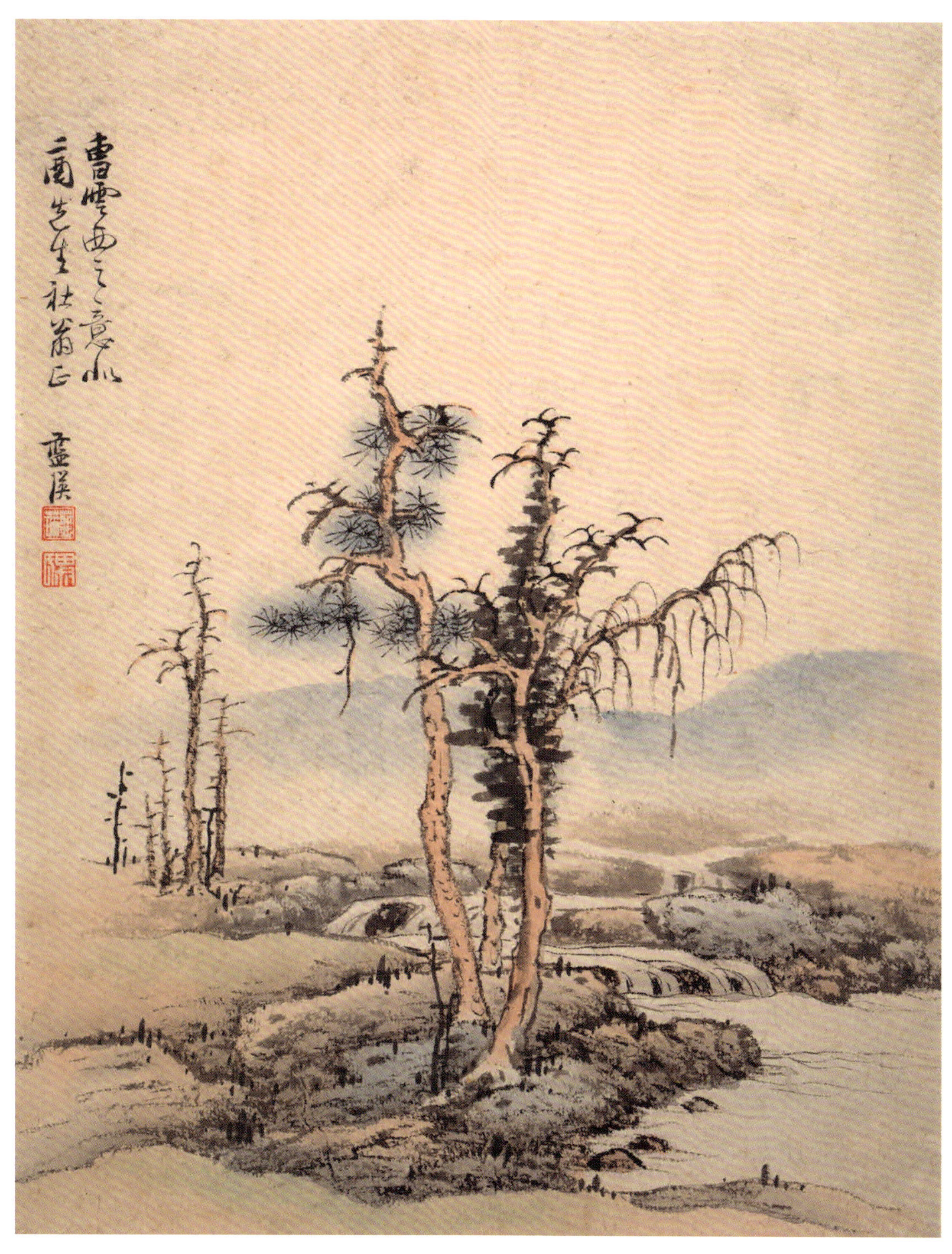

黄隺山樵画

壬午春正月
藍溪畫

277. 仿高克恭云林秋霁图

明崇祯十五年（公元1642年）
蓝瑛
纸本设色
册页
纵31、横40.7厘米
芝加哥艺术博物馆

Landscape After Gao Kegong

Ming dynasty (1368–1644), dated 1642
Lan Ying
Ink and color on paper
Album leaf
H×W : 31×40.7 cm
The Art Institute of Chicago
Samuel M. Nickerson fund

278. 仿王蒙山水图

明崇祯十五年（公元1642年）
蓝瑛
纸本设色
册页
纵31、横40.7厘米
芝加哥艺术博物馆

Landscape After Wang Meng

Ming dynasty (1368–1644), dated 1642
Lan Ying
Ink and color on paper
Album leaf
H×W : 31×40.7 cm
The Art Institute of Chicago
Samuel M. Nickerson fund

279. 仿赵孟頫山水图

明崇祯十五年（公元1642年）
蓝瑛
纸本设色
册页
纵31、横40.7厘米
芝加哥艺术博物馆

Landscape After Zhao Mengfu

Ming dynasty (1368–1644), dated 1642
Lan Ying
Ink and color on paper
Album leaf
H×W : 31×40.7 cm
The Art Institute of Chicago
Samuel M. Nickerson fund

280. 冬日山居图

清顺治六年（公元1649年）
蓝瑛
绢本设色
立轴
纵183、横68.1厘米
明尼阿波利斯美术馆

Thatched Huts Among Ridges in Winter

Late Ming to early Qing dynasty, dated 1649
Lan Ying
Ink and color on silk
Hanging scroll
H×W : 183×68.1 cm
The Minneapolis Institute of Art
Gift of Joan Wurtele

281. 秋山图

Autumn Landscape

清顺治十年（公元1653年）
蓝瑛
绢本设色
立轴
纵194.3、横48.9厘米
耶鲁大学艺术博物馆

Late Ming to early Qing dynasty, dated 1653
Lan Ying
Ink and color on silk
Hanging scroll
H×W : 194.3×48.9 cm
The Yale University Art Gallery
Anonymous gift in honor of Professor Nelson Wu

282. 仿李唐山水图

明
蓝瑛
纸本设色
立轴
纵173.5、横55.9厘米
耶鲁大学艺术博物馆

Landscape After Li Tang

Ming dynasty (1368–1644)
Lan Ying
Ink and color on paper
Hanging scroll
H×W : 173.5×55.9 cm
The Yale University Art Gallery
Gift of Kathleen and Denis C. Yang

283. 楚山秋霁图

明
蓝瑛
绢本设色
立轴
纵185.3、横48.4厘米
克利夫兰美术馆

Clearing Autumn Mists in Chu Mountains

Ming dynasty (1368–1644)
Lan Ying
Ink and color on silk
Hanging scroll
H×W : 185.3×48.4 cm
The Cleveland Museum of Art
Purchase from the J. H. Wade Fund 1971.231

284. 论道图

明
蓝瑛
纸本水墨
立轴
纵141、横56厘米
克利夫兰美术馆

Conversation

Ming dynasty (1368–1644)
Lan Ying
Ink on paper
Hanging scroll
H×W : 141×56 cm
The Cleveland Museum of Art
Gift of Stephen O. K. Chen 1970.128

紅友

285. 红友图

Red Friend

明清之际
蓝瑛
纸本设色
立轴
纵148.9、横47.3厘米
大都会艺术博物馆

Late Ming to early Qing dynasty
Lan Ying
Ink and color on paper
Hanging scroll
H×W : 148.9×47.3 cm
The Metropolitan Museum of Art
Ex coll.: C. C. Wang Family, Gift of Mr. and Mrs. Earl Morse, in honor of Douglas Dillon, 1979

286. 仿李成山水图

Autumn colors at Mountain Villa After Li Cheng

明清之际
蓝瑛
绢本设色
立轴
纵175.2、横76.5厘米
哈佛艺术博物馆

Late Ming to early Qing dynasty
Lan Ying
Ink and color on silk
Hanging scroll
H×W : 175.2×76.5 cm
The Harvard Art Museums
Harvard Art Museums/Arthur M. Sackler Museum,
Edward B. Bruce Collection of Chinese Paintings;
Gift of Galen L. Stone

287. 仿王维山水图

明清之际
蓝瑛
绢本设色
立轴
纵163.3、横46.7厘米
波士顿美术博物馆

Landscape After Wang Wei

Late Ming to early Qing dynasty
Lan Ying
Ink and color on silk
Hanging scroll
H×W : 163.3×46.7 cm
The Museum of Fine Arts, Boston
Chinese and Japanese Special Fund
15.895

288. 桃园春色图

Peach Blossom Spring

清顺治七年（公元1650年）
刘度
绫本设色
立轴
纵135.8、横52厘米
克利夫兰美术馆

Late Ming to early Qing dynasty, dated 1650
Liu Du
Ink and color on satin
Hanging scroll
H×W : 135.8×52 cm
The Cleveland Museum of Art
John L. Severance Fund 1971.227

289. 仿巨然山水图

明清之际
（传）刘度
绢本设色
立轴
纵169.5、横105.1厘米
克利夫兰美术馆

Landscape After Ju Ran

Late Ming to early Qing dynasty
Attributed to Liu Du
Ink and color on silk
Hanging scroll
H×W : 169.5×105.1 cm
The Cleveland Museum of Art
Gift of the John Huntington Art and Polytechnic Trust 1915.621

290. 仿古山水图

明崇祯八年（公元1635年）
魏之克
纸本设色
手卷
纵32.1、横1183.6厘米
大都会艺术博物馆

Landscape After Old Masters

Ming dynasty (1368–1644), dated 1635
Wei Zhike
Ink and color on paper
Handscroll
H×W : 32.1×1183.6 cm
The Metropolitan Museum of Art
Gift of J. T. Tai, 1968

崇禎乙亥二月寫

291. 秋江落照图

明清之际
潘云驭
纸本设色
册页
纵15.9、横48.3厘米
大都会艺术博物馆

Setting Sun on Autumn River

Late Ming to early Qing dynasty
Pan Yunyu
Ink and color on paper
Album leaf
H×W : 15.9×48.3 cm
The Metropolitan Museum of Art
John Stewart Kennedy Fund, 1913

292. 许旌阳移居图

明崇祯十七年（公元1644年）
崔子忠
绢本设色
立轴
纵268.2、横66厘米
克利夫兰美术馆

Xu Jingyang Moving His Family

Ming dynasty (1368–1644), dated 1644
Cui Zizhong
Ink and color on silk
Hanging scroll
H×W : 268.2×66 cm
The Cleveland Museum of Art
Mr. and Mrs. William H. Marlatt Fund 1961.90

293. 洗象图

明
（传）崔子忠
绫本设色
立轴
纵124.3、横52.1厘米
弗利尔美术馆

Grooming Elephant

Ming dynasty (1368–1644)
Attributed to Cui Zizhong
Ink and color on satin
Hanging scroll
H×W : 124.3×52.1 cm
The Freer Gallery of Art
Gift of Charles Lang Freer

版权支持

（按中文馆名音序排列）

鲍尔基金会鲍氏东方艺术馆
贝纳基博物馆
波士顿艺术博物馆
不列颠博物馆
大阪市立东洋陶瓷美术馆
大阪市立美术馆
大都会艺术博物馆
东京国立博物馆
费城艺术博物馆
菲尔德博物馆
弗利尔美术馆
弗利尔与赛克勒美术馆
哈佛艺术博物馆
荷兰国立博物馆
集美博物馆
金贝尔艺术博物馆
凯布朗利博物馆
克利夫兰艺术博物馆
科隆东亚艺术博物馆
洛杉矶郡艺术博物馆
明尼阿波利斯美术馆
奈良国立博物馆
普林斯顿大学美术馆
赛克勒博物馆
赛克勒美术馆
圣路易斯艺术博物馆
维多利亚和阿尔伯特博物馆
新南威尔士州美术馆
辛辛那提艺术博物馆
亚洲文明博物馆
耶鲁大学艺术博物馆
印第安纳波利斯艺术博物馆
芝加哥艺术博物馆

Image Contributors

(In Chinese Pinyin Order)

The Baur Foundation, Museum of Far Eastern Art
The Benaki Museum
The Museum of Fine Arts, Boston
The British Museum
The Museum of Oriental Ceramics, Osaka
The Osaka City Museum of Fine Arts
The Metropolitan Museum of Art
The Tokyo National Museum
The Philadelphia Museum of Art
The Field Museum
The Freer Gallery of Art
The Freer and the Arthur M. Sackler Gallery
The Harvard Art Museums
The Rijksmuseum
The Guimet Museum
The Kimbell Art Museum
The Quai Branly Museum
The Cleveland Museum of Art
The Museum of East Asian Art, Cologne
The Los Angeles County Museum of Art
The Minneapolis Institute of Art
The Nara National Museum
The Princeton University Art Museum
The Arthur M. Sackler Museum
The Arthur M. Sackler Gallery
The Saint Louis Art Museum
The Victoria and Albert Museum
The Art Gallery of New South Wales
The Cincinnati Art Museum
The Asian Civilisations Museum
The Yale University Art Gallery
The Indianapolis Museum of Art
The Art Institute of Chicago

编辑、出版人员

总 策 划　马汝军　谢　刚
选题策划　孙志鹏
主任编辑　邹懿男
出版统筹　丁　宁

责任编辑　李文彧　林　琳
特约编辑　丁文文
编　　辑　陈　雯　张小君　汪　欣　孙立英　白华召　施　然　马　源
　　　　　赵笑笑　刘　琦　黄　艳　王　萌　王颖洁　王宏亮　毕力格图
责任校对　刘　义
实习编辑　齐倩颖　潘泓瑾

英文翻译　丁文文　耿玮浩
英文审校　韩　华

装帧设计　冷暖儿
图文版式　魏　丹　杨　丹　阮鸽鸽
责任印制　韦　舰　李珊珊